An Outdoor Family Guide to

YELLOWSTONE & GRAND TETON

NATIONAL PARKS

Lisa Gollin Evans

THE
MOUNTAINEERS

To Frank, with love and gratitude

 Published by
The Mountaineers
1001 SW Klickitat Way, Suite 201
Seattle, Washington 98134

First edition: first printing 1996, revised 1998, third printing 2000, fourth printing 2002

Published simultaneously in Great Britain by Cordee, 3a DeMontfort Street, Leicester, England, LE1 7HD

Manufactured in the United States of America

Edited by Paula Thurman
Maps by Jerry Painter
All photographs by the author
Cover design by Watson Graphics
Art for chapter openings by Sarah and Gracie Evans
Book design by Bridget Culligan
Book layout by Virginia Hand
Cover photographs: Ned Strong and Lisa Gollin Evans

Library of Congress Cataloging-in-Publication Data

Evans, Lisa Gollin, 1956–
    An outdoor family guide to Yellowstone & Grand Teton National Parks / Lisa Gollin Evans.
        p.   cm.
    Includes bibliographical references and index.
    ISBN 0-89886-428-3
    1. Hiking—Yellowstone National Park—Guidebooks. 2. Hiking—Wyoming —Grand Teton National Park—Guidebooks. 3. Cycling—Yellowstone National Park—Guidebooks. 4. Cycling—Wyoming—Grand Teton National Park—Guidebooks. 5. Boats and boating—Yellowstone National Park— Guidebooks. 6. Boats and boating—Wyoming—Grand Teton National Park— Guidebooks. 7. Family recreation. 8. Yellowstone National Park—Guidebooks. 9. Grand Teton National Park Wyo.—Guidebooks. I. Title.
GV199.42.Y45E92   1996
917.87'52—dc20   95–51254

                                                                    CIP

Contents

Legend

(T) Trailhead	✕ Canoe portage	🚻 Restroom
(P) Parking	■ Building or site	➕ Clinic
⌃ Peak	(89) U.S. highway	🛏 Lodging
(↺) Turnaround	(30) State highway	$ Store
⅂⎺ Picnic area	▬ Paved roadway	Gas
📷 Viewpoint	═ Dirt or gravel road	FS Full services
(PI) Put-in	- - - - Main trail	▲ Campground
(TO) Take out	- - - - Secondary trail	Boat dock
⌇ Bridge	◠ Water	Visitor center/ ranger station

Preface

The Greater Yellowstone Ecosystem is one of the best destinations in the country for vacationing families. Within its borders, two national parks, Yellowstone and Grand Teton, offer rich recreation as well as unparalleled beauty. Limitless blue sky, wide open spaces, and abundant wildlife fill its wilderness. From eagles to bison, hot springs to waterfalls, precipitous peaks to plunging canyons, the parks' natural wonders are marvelously accessible.

Nevertheless, a word of warning: Don't attempt to "do" the whole of Yellowstone and Grand Teton in a day, or even two. Eight hours on a traffic-clogged road is a mind-numbing experience and a surefire way to generate cranky kids, headaches, and poor memories. This book offers an alternative to the "drive-thru" tour. It reveals incredibly beautiful places to stroll, hike, swim, bike, paddle, view wildlife, and learn about the wilderness.

With the aid of this book, leave your car and discover a part of the earth largely unchanged by man. Enter a world where you are no longer the dominant predator; where hot, hissing steam rises from the ground; where you are watched by a hundred unseen eyes; where extremes of height and depth, hot and cold, beauty and ghastliness are beyond your control and imagination. This is a land of wonderment: of 90,000 elk, 4,000 bison, and hundreds of grizzlies, black bear, antelope, and moose.

But what about the hordes of humans? The traffic jams? The souvenir shops and sprawling campgrounds? Admittedly, these things are there, but it is easy to avoid them. Two hundred feet down any trail and the parking lot and traffic noise are unseen, unheard, and forgotten.

For families, the lure of a national park is not only its wildness, but the quality of its interpretive services and the accessibility of its adventures. The park service at Yellowstone and Grand Teton offers a rich array of ranger-led hikes, campfire programs, junior ranger opportunities, and informative visitor centers. For family adventures, the mix is broad and enticing, including well-marked trails, scenic campsites, world-famous trout streams, gentle lakes, and an abundance of horses, rafts, and kayaks for hire.

Take your family to Yellowstone. You won't regret it.

Acknowledgments

I'd like to express special and sincere thanks to all those who made this book a joy to write; my favorite hiking partners, Frank, Sarah, and Grace; my mother, Hannah Gollin, who is always a source of strength and wisdom; my father, Morton Gollin, who can *still* beat me in tennis and can still hike the trails; my wonderful father-in-law and mother-in-law, Frank and Anne Evans; two terrific nieces, Kerry Sullivan and Kristen O'Connell; and my most excellent friends: Ned, Julie, Peter, and Catherine Strong; Patty, Zac, and Sara Yoffe; and last (but not least) Dan, Allyn, Katie, and Nancy Carl.

I'd also like to thank the many helpful rangers and naturalists of Yellowstone and Grand Teton National parks who provided invaluable assistance. Particularly, I'd like to express special thanks to park naturalist Peter Dederich of Grand Teton, who patiently and expertly answered my endless questions.

Appreciation is also due to Gene Ball, former director of the Yellowstone Institute, who taught me indispensible lessons on wildlife observation, and to the following outfitters, *par excellence:* Far and Away Adventures, the Teton Crest Outfitters, and O.A.R.S., who brought me wonderful places I might never have seen.

Lastly, I want to thank Dr. Patricia Moody for the generous and lengthy loan of her bear bells, which helped to keep me and my family safe and sound in the backcountry.

Lisa Gollin Evans

Introduction

This book describes forty-eight hiking, biking, and boating outings chosen specifically for families. Each outing introduces parents and children to natural features of the park, and each description alerts them to animals, plants, thermal features, and more that they might otherwise miss. To get the most out of your visit, the book also includes detailed information on the parks' interpretive resources, camping, horseback riding, fishing, boating, wildlife viewing, and other activities in and near the parks. Yellowstone and Grand Teton are full of adventures for visiting families; this book is full of easy ways to make them happen.

How to Use this Book

Before setting out on any outing, consult this Introduction for tips on hiking, biking and boating with children; safety considerations; wilderness ethics; park regulations; and essential equipment. More specific information on Yellowstone and Grand Teton, including campgrounds, lodging, weather, natural history, and recreational opportunities, is discussed in Chapter 1.

Following Chapter 1 are forty-eight detailed trip descriptions, organized by geographic region. The outings are classified as easy, moderate, or strenuous, according to their length, starting elevation, elevation gain, and terrain. Generally, easy trips are 0.5 to 2 miles one way, moderate trips are 2 to 4 miles one way, and strenuous trips are over 4 miles one way. To help you quickly choose an outing that fits your needs, appendix A contains a trip matrix that concisely lists information such as difficulty, distance, elevation gain, location, and attractions. Also included in these descriptions are symbols that indicate whether the trip is a hike, bike, or paddle, and whether backcountry camping is available.

The trail descriptions do not provide estimates of walking or biking time. Hikers and bikers, especially children, travel at such variable speeds that general approximations would not be reliable. To roughly estimate the time required for a hike, use the average walking rate of 2 miles per hour on level ground for adults carrying packs, plus 1 hour for each 1,000 feet of elevation gained.

Difficult terrain and hiking children obviously increase the time needed. After a few hikes, you can work out estimates for your own family. Generally, strenuous hikes require a full day; moderate hikes, a half day; and easy hikes, 1 to 3 hours.

Several appendixes follow the outing descriptions. Appendix B contains a wildlife locator indicating the most likely places to view wildlife, as well as suggestions for self-guided "wildlife safaris." Appendix C contains a bibliography for children and adults with recommended books on the area's natural and regional history. Lastly, appendix D provides information on conservation organizations working to protect the Greater Yellowstone Ecosystem.

Tips on Hiking, Biking, and Paddling with Children

CHOOSING THE RIGHT TRIP

Hiking, biking, or paddling a route that's too difficult for your children is sure to lead to frustration for all. Read trip descriptions carefully to find outings that match your children's abilities. If you are uncertain how far they can go, choose a trip that has intermediate points of interest, so that you can shorten it if necessary. Try also to match your youngsters' interests with an outing's particular attractions, whether they be fishing, rock climbing, swimming, or wildflowers.

SNACKS

Let children snack liberally on their favorite treats while on an outing. They will be working hard, and snacks high in carbohydrates and sugar boost their energy. Also, salty snacks are good for replacing salts lost through perspiration. Good-tasting treats can also be used as a motivating force for reaching the next rest stop. Don't forget to bring plenty of water or juice, particularly in summer, when humidity is low and temperatures are high. Mild dehydration causes crankiness in children, and more severe cases can cause extreme discomfort.

MOTIVATION

There are numerous ways to motivate children. The promise of a picnic or a treat is enough for some. For others, encouraging good-natured competition with siblings or peers does the trick. When a child's motivation wears thin, distraction can be the best solution. Songs, trail activities, games, and stories often invigorate sluggish youngsters. Consult appendix C for books containing trail activities.

LEADERS

Allow children to lead the group. When the novelty wears off, assign the lead role to another, rotating the honor among the youngsters. Let children determine the pace. Progress may be slower than desired, but the trip will be much more enjoyable. Adults will also benefit from slowing down: you may cover only half the distance, but you'll experience twice as much.

POSITIVE ATTITUDE

Praise children for all their achievements on the trail. Positive reinforcement for beginners is essential to build a solid base of good feelings about nature outings. Refrain from criticism if children disappoint you. Scolding won't improve their performance; it will only guarantee unhappiness.

THE RIGHT STUFF

Pack items in your backpack to keep children happy on the trail, especially when hiking. Magnifying glasses, binoculars, cameras, junior field guides, bug bottles, sketchbooks, or materials for simple projects like bark and stone rubbings provide welcome diversions for youngsters who need a break. A child-sized walking stick can also provide miles of enjoyment for a young hiker.

RELAX

When hiking, biking, and paddling with children, the joy is in the process, in the small achievements and discoveries you share. To appreciate this, you must relax. You may miss the thrill of a peak or the rush of rapids, but the quiet rewards of sharing nature last a lifetime and build a foundation for your next trip.

Wilderness Ethics

To keep the parks healthy and the wildlife safe, it is essential that visitors follow a simple code of wilderness ethics.

MAKE A POSITIVE IMPACT

The rule of Positive Impact goes beyond the oft-repeated "Take only pictures; leave only footprints." That maxim falls short in today's overcrowded parks. My rule of Positive Impact asks that visitors leave the park a *better* place. By picking up waste, for example, you enhance the beauty of the trail for the next visitor. Give children a small bag to stuff in their pocket for their own litter as well as for stray wrappers left by others. Parents should carry litter bags, too.

A second way to create a positive impact is to set a good example by hiking, biking, and paddling joyfully, attentively, and considerately. The model will be contagious. Just as a crowd gathers to look at a sight in which others show interest, other visitors will follow your lead if you find a trail interesting, fun, or exhilarating.

DO NOT FEED THE ANIMALS

Do not feed the small mammals and birds who beg for handouts. Feeding is dangerous for you *and* the animals. Human food harms wildlife in several ways. First, snack foods are a poor

Backcountry Campsite Guidelines

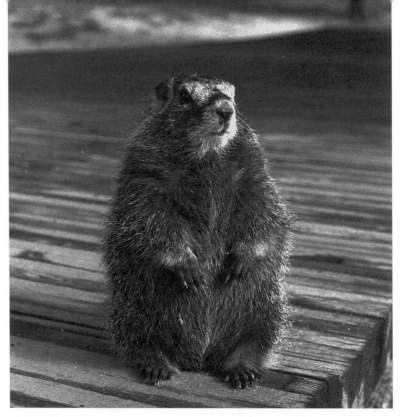

Yellow-bellied marmot

nutritional substitute for an animal's natural diet. If handouts become a primary source of food, the animal may become malnourished and prey to disease and injury. Second, feeding an animal disrupts its natural foraging instincts. As a result, animals who depend on human feeding may not survive the winter. Third, human feeding unnaturally concentrates animal populations. An unusually large population of marmots or ground squirrels at a picnic area leaves that population vulnerable to epidemic disease.

Feeding wild animals is also dangerous for people. Small mammals may carry rabies, a potentially lethal disease. Rabies aside, a rodent's sharp incisors in your finger is painful. Second, fleas carrying bubonic plague have been found on the park's rodents. Although rare, instances of human contraction of bubonic plague from flea bites have occurred.

PROTECT AND RESPECT THE BEARS

Protect the parks' bears by storing your food correctly while camping. Bears that successfully raid campsites often end up dead.

Once a bear associates people with food, it continues to frequent campgrounds. The park service relocates food-habituated bears, but they often return. Unnatural feeding behavior inevitably places bears in close proximity to people, where unfortunate encounters are likely. If a food-conditioned bear injures a person, the park service may be forced to destroy it. Avoid this sad chain of events by securing food and garbage properly. By hanging food, using backcountry storage boxes, and utilizing your car trunk, you can save a bear's life (see diagram on page 19).

Respect closures and restrictions in Yellowstone's Bear Management Areas (BMAs). Periodically, the National Park Service (NPS) designates a backcountry area as a BMA to reduce human impact in high-density grizzly bear habitat. The park service may close an area entirely or restrict it to day use. These periodic closures are essential to protect Yellowstone's threatened grizzly population. Before hiking, inquire about bear closures at a visitor center or ranger station. In addition, look for NPS postings at the trailhead. If a bear is sighted while hiking or camping, report your sighting at the nearest ranger station or visitor center.

LET WILDFLOWERS FLOURISH

From May through September, wild gardens grace the Greater Yellowstone Ecosystem. To ensure that all have an opportunity to enjoy the flowers, visitors must refrain from picking even one blossom. At high elevations, picking wildflowers poses a particularly critical problem because plants have little time in which to set seed. Removing plants means removing seeds, thus preventing annuals from reproducing. This may have a dire impact on the food supply for the park's wildlife.

STAY ON THE TRAIL

To maintain the integrity, beauty, and safety of trails, do not shortcut. Shortcuts are most tempting where a trail switchbacks down a steep slope. When hikers aim straight down a slope, they damage the vegetation between the switchbacks and cause erosion. If shortcutting occurs frequently, a trail may wash away, leaving a scarred and barren hillside. Also, abandoning a trail on a precipitous slope is dangerous and may cause one to fall or lose the trail entirely.

OBSERVE PARK RULES

Written copies of NPS regulations are available at ranger stations and visitor centers. A few of the most important, and most commonly violated, are the following:

- Carry out all refuse. Leave no waste on trails or in campsites. Do not attempt to burn or bury noncombustibles.
- Do not cut, remove, deface, or disturb any tree, shrub, wildflower, or other natural object. Carving on trees scars them permanently and can even kill them if the carving girdles the tree.
- Use only dead and downed wood for firewood. Never break branches from standing trees, even if they appear dead. The tree may still be living, and breaking a branch may injure it.
- Removal of rocks, minerals, fossils, or cultural artifacts from the park is prohibited.
- Collecting antlers and animal bones is also prohibited. Bones and antlers are an important source of minerals for the park's smaller animals.
- Edible plants, mushrooms, and berries may only be picked for your daily consumption. *Do not* eat any plants that you can't positively identify. Poisonous plants grow in both parks!
- All hunting is prohibited, as are firearms.
- Fishing requires a fishing permit for those over 11 years of age. Permits are available at ranger stations and visitor centers.
- Pets are prohibited on trails, in the backcountry, on boardwalks, and in thermal areas. Pets are allowed only within 25 feet of roads and parking areas and must be leashed.
- A permit is required for all boats and a Coast Guard-approved flotation device is required for each person boating.
- Do not alter or put any objects in thermal features. These features are easily clogged and hence destroyed after tampering.

BUILDERS BEWARE

Don't build *anything* in the park. Don't build cairns, fireplaces, benches, or soft places to sleep. These structures linger long after you've left and blight the landscape. When camping, "naturalize" your camp before leaving by making the site look as if no one had camped there. Then make a positive impact by packing out any waste left by previous campers.

GET THE LEAD OUT

Beginning in 1994, Yellowstone National Park began a lead-free fishing program. Wildlife such as loons, cranes, shorebirds, and trumpeter swans are particularly vulnerable to lead poisoning. As a result, the park prohibits fishing tackle such as leaded split-shot sinkers, weighted jigs (lead-molded to a hook), and soft lead-weighted ribbon.

BIKE RESPONSIBLY

Bicycles are prohibited on backcountry trails and on board-walks in the national parks. Bicycling is permitted only on established public roads and a few designated routes. Ask a ranger for a list of routes open to bicycles.

LIGHT STOVES, NOT FIRES

In the backcountry, small fires are permitted at specific campsites within existing fire rings. Even where fires are allowed, the

Kayaking on Jackson Lake, Grand Teton National Park

NPS discourages wood fires and recommends portable cooking stoves. Fires leave unsightly scars on the land, rob forests of decomposing matter, present hazards in drought-stricken areas, and create haze in pristine skies. Also, ash carried by runoff contaminates lakes and streams. If you feel you can't camp without a fire, make it small, don't use it for cooking, limit its duration ,and extinguish it carefully. Lastly, to make a positive impact, dismantle extra fire rings by scattering the rocks and condense overly large fire rings to discourage big fires.

PROTECT THE LAKES

Backcountry lakes and streams are fragile and easily damaged by careless visitors. To protect them, set up camp, eliminate waste, and wash dishes at least 100 feet away. If picnicking on a lake shore, choose a boulder or use areas already heavily impacted. It is unlikely that highly impacted areas will recover, and you will avoid spreading the damage. In addition, don't use any soaps in or near lakes and streams, because *all* soaps pollute, even those that claim to be biodegradable.

Safety Tips for Yellowstone and Grand Teton National Parks

This section summarizes the basic precautions to be taken when visiting Yellowstone and Grand Teton national parks. Be alert to the dangers described below and be prepared with the appropriate knowledge and gear to minimize hazardous situations. The checklist at the end of this section lists the essentials you need to take on *every* outing.

BEARS

The Greater Yellowstone Ecosystem is home to black bears and grizzly bears. Sighting a bear is one of the parks' greatest thrills, but it also brings grave risks. All bears are unpredictable and potentially lethal. As a result, visitors should avoid bear confrontations and know what to do if one occurs.

Bear attacks are primarily caused by four occurrences: (1) surprising a bear; (2) getting between a sow and her cubs; (3) approaching a carcass or a bear with food, and (4) approaching a bear for a photo. To avoid placing yourself or your family in one of these dangerous situations, the NPS advises that visitors take the following precautions:

- *Be alert.* Learn how to recognize bear signs, including tracks, scat, and diggings. Use binoculars to scan the terrain while hiking. Fleeing wildlife may indicate the presence of bears; spotting a cub means there is a sow nearby.
- *Make noise.* The more noise you make, the less likely you are to surprise a bear. Talk, sing, clap hands, and shake pebbles in a can. Don't rely on bear bells alone. Shout when entering dense and brushy vegetation, when traveling near noisy streams, and when hiking upwind. Whistling is not recommended because you may unwittingly sound like another animal and actually attract a bear!
- *Travel in groups of five or more.* Large parties are safer because they make more noise and are better able to effect a rescue in case of an emergency. Do not hike alone or allow children to be separated from the group.
- *Don't hike at night.* Bears travel and feed primarily at night. Plan your day so that your hiking is complete by dusk. Poor light increases your chances of surprising a bear.
- *Avoid carcasses.* Don't approach a dead elk, bison, or any other animal carcass. A bear may be out of sight guarding its food. Stop if you smell rotting meat while hiking. Other signs of carcasses include concentrations of ravens and/or coyotes. Never camp near a carcass. For the protection of others, report any dead animal near a trail or campsite to the nearest ranger station.
- *Avoid smelly food.* Don't bring odorous food into the backcountry. Bears have a legendary sense of smell and can even smell tuna in an unopened can! While camping: (1) keep a clean camp, (2) use food poles where provided, (3) don't sleep in the same clothes worn while cooking, (4) never store food or eat in your tent, (5) store food in airtight containers, (6) keep your sleeping area at least 100 yards from your cooking/food storage area, (7) bring at least 50 feet of rope to hang food, (8) hang food 10 feet from the ground and 4 feet out from tree trunks, and (9) don't bring large containers such as ice chests unless you're prepared to hang them. Also avoid wearing fragrant deodorants, sunscreens, or perfumes.

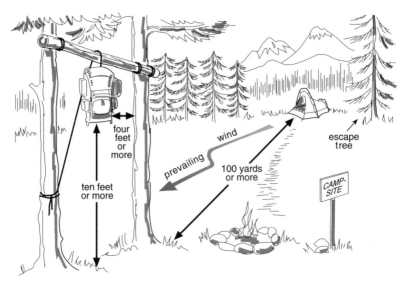

Guidelines for Food Storage in bear country

Despite all the above precautions, you might still see a bear. In that event, the NPS recommends:

- *If you see a bear at a distance:* Keep out of sight and detour as far away as possible. *Do not run.* By running, you will attract the attention of the bear, and you might be pursued. *You cannot outrun a bear.* Bears can sprint up to 40 miles per hour. If the bear sees you but is still quite a distance away, you can climb a tree *if* you can climb at least 15 feet up and preferably higher. Remember that all black bears, grizzly cubs, and even some adult grizzlies can climb trees if the spacing of the branches is right.
- *If you encounter a bear at close range:* Back away slowly, dropping gear or clothing if possible. Talk quietly to the bear. *Do not run or make sudden movements.* Avoid looking directly at the bear. Move your arms up and down slowly at your sides. Be prepared for a charge.
- *If a bear charges:* Freeze, *never run.* Many charges are "bluff charges." Bears may charge and then veer off or stop at the last second. If the bear does not stop, *play dead.* Drop to the ground, lift your legs to your chest, clasp the back of your neck, and protect your head. Your pack will shield your body. Bears have been known to inflict only minor injuries under

these circumstances. Lie still and silent, for resistance would be useless. Be sure the bear is gone before moving.

- *Night attacks in your tent:* In this instance, *be aggressive and defend yourself. Do not play dead!* The bear in this situation is being predatory, so you must let the bear know that you are not easy prey. If the "prey" is too troublesome, the bear will give up. Develop with others in your party a course of action should this rare situation arise.

- *If you observe a bear prowling around the perimeter of your campsite:* Do not go to sleep. Climb a tree, if possible, and be prepared to stay in the tree until daylight. Then hike back to the trailhead and report the incident to a ranger immediately so that the campsite can be closed.

Lastly, for the safety of all park visitors, report all bear sightings and bear signs (scat, tracks, fresh carcasses) to the nearest park ranger.

Chemical bear repellents: Some professionals carry aerosol canisters of capsaicin, an irritant made from cayenne pepper. Tests have shown that when sprayed in the eyes, a bear will immediately retreat. This is not, by any means, a foolproof solution to bear encounters. Bears are highly unpredictable, and it is possible that spraying could incite a more aggressive attack. In addition, the spray has a very limited range, is subject to wind conditions, and must be aimed accurately in a moment of intense stress. If you're considering carrying a canister, read all warnings and practice before setting out.

WILDLIFE

Keep a safe distance from all wildlife. Park regulations prohibit approaching within 25 yards of wildlife and within 100 yards of bears. All park animals are unpredictable and dangerous. Bison are especially aggressive. Each year, bison inflict severe injuries on visitors who approach too closely. Be wary of any large animal with young. Elk, moose, and deer may also show aggression and cause grave injury during their mating seasons. In addition, for your safety, drive defensively on park roads, particularly between dusk and dawn. Large animals, especially bison, also use the roadways.

THERMAL FEATURES

Stay on boardwalks and designated trails when viewing thermal features. The crust around these features may be thin, and a misstep could plunge you into boiling water. Also, use extreme caution when frost glazes wooden boardwalks, for they become slippery.

Never swim in thermal pools or streams whose waters flow entirely from a thermal spring. It is illegal and hazardous. In addition, many thermal springs and pools are extremely acidic or alkaline. Each year some visitors are badly burned. Thermal waters may also contain organisms known to cause infections and/or amoebic meningitis, which can be fatal.

HYPOTHERMIA

To avoid hypothermia, hikers must always be prepared for sudden mountain storms. Hypothermia is the lowering of the body's core temperature to a degree sufficient to cause illness. The condition is serious and sometimes fatal. Signs of mild hypothermia include complaints of coldness, shivering, loss of coordination, and apathy. More severe hypothermia causes mental confusion, uncontrollable shivering, slurred speech, and a core temperature low enough to cause permanent damage or death.

Because small bodies lose heat more rapidly than large ones, children are more vulnerable to hypothermia than adults. Early signs of hypothermia in children may be crankiness and fussiness, which can also be caused by ordinary fatigue. A child might not even realize he or she is cold until serious shivering begins. Hikers, especially children, can become hypothermic when temperatures are well above freezing. Wind chill is a critical, and often overlooked, cause of hypothermia.

Parents can guard against dangerous chills by observing the following precautions:

- Carry an adequate supply of warm clothing, including wool sweaters, socks, gloves, and hats to insulate against heat loss. Gloves, hats, and scarves are particularly effective because they protect hands, heads, and necks—areas that are especially sensitive to heat loss. Carry these items even when the weather looks warm and sunny, especially at or above tree line. On cool rainy days, avoid cotton clothing, which is not warm when wet and wicks warmth away from the body.
- Dress in layers and remove unneeded layers to prevent excessive sweating, which lowers body temperature through evaporation. Parents must react quickly to temperature

changes, whether occasioned by weather or changes in activity levels.

- Put on raingear *before* you get wet, and put on warm clothes before shivering begins.
- Avoid excessive exposure to wind and rain. *Always* carry raingear.
- Carry food high in carbohydrates and sugar that the body can quickly convert to heat.
- Carry warm liquids, such as hot cocoa, when hiking in cold weather.
- Avoid resting against ice, snow, or cold rocks, which draw heat away from the body. Place an insulating barrier, such as a foam pad, between the body and cold surfaces.
- Cover the mouth with a wool scarf to warm air entering the lungs.

If a member of your group shows signs of hypothermia, stop and take immediate steps to warm the person. Promptness is critical when treating hypothermia in children. Add layers of clothing. Replace wet clothes with dry ones. If possible, administer warm liquids or food. If necessary, build a small fire to warm the victim and dry wet clothing. Holding a cold child close to your body while wrapping a parka or blanket around the two of you is particularly effective. Crawling into a sleeping bag with the victim is recommended for cases that do not respond readily to other treatment.

HEAT-RELATED ILLNESS AND SUN EXPOSURE

Hiking, biking, or paddling at high altitudes, in warm weather, or in the open sun can cause excessive loss of water and salts (electrolytes). Failure to replace water and electrolytes can lead to dehydration, heat exhaustion, or even heat stroke. To prevent heat-related illnesses, consume adequate amounts of water and electrolytes. Avoid salt tablets in favor of salted snacks and liquids, which you should carry in amounts greater than you are likely to need. Flavored powders containing electrolytes may be added to water to replace those lost through perspiration. Remember that thirst is not a reliable indicator of the need for water. Schedule regular water stops to ensure against dehydration.

Precautions against over-exposure to the sun are necessary in any season. During the dry, sunny summers, it is particularly important to avoid excessive exposure, especially on summit hikes. Harmful ultraviolet radiation increases with altitude. Also take

Girl and horse, Yellowstone National Park

additional precautions when in or near lakes, for radiation reflects off bodies of water.

HAZARDS OF HIGH ALTITUDE—MOUNTAIN SICKNESS

Road elevations in Yellowstone National Park range from 5,300 to 8,860 feet. In Grand Teton National Park, most trails start around 6,800 feet. The decreased oxygen in the air at high altitudes can result in mountain sickness. Symptoms include headaches, fatigue, loss of appetite, weakness and dull pain in muscles, shortness of breath, nausea, and rapid heartbeat. If ignored or left untreated, mountain sickness can be fatal.

Mountain sickness strikes unpredictably. It affects both young and old, whether fit or not. Some people may experience no symptoms on one day but quickly develop them on another. In any case, the cardinal rule when the early symptoms of mountain sickness appear is to descend at once to a lower elevation.

To reduce the likelihood of mountain sickness, acclimate your family to high altitude gradually. At the beginning of your visit, choose trips at the lowest altitude, or at least, those in the high country that are not strenuous. Because children are often inarticulate about their physical condition, be attuned to crankiness as a sign of altitude discomfort. If suspected, rest and retreat to lower elevations as soon as possible. To aid the family's acclimation, make sure everyone eats lightly, drinks plenty of fluids, gets sufficient rest, and limits physical activity for the first few days. Adults should limit their intake of alcohol at high elevations.

LIGHTNING

Deep blue skies and low humidity are typical throughout the summer and fall in the Greater Yellowstone Ecosystem. The afternoons, however, are frequently interrupted by sudden thunderstorms, particularly in July and August. If you are hiking on an open ridge, above tree line, or in an open area with few trees, you may be in danger of being hit by lightning, because lightning strikes at the highest object. If you do get caught in a thunderstorm, take the following precautions:

- Do *not* seek shelter under natural features, such as lone or tall trees, rock overhangs, or large boulders which project above their surroundings. Such large, exposed objects are more likely to be hit by lightning because of their height.
- Do *not* lie flat on the ground. To do so is to increase the body area exposed to electrical current in the event of a nearby strike.
- Assume the safest position—huddle on your knees with your head down. Crouch near medium-sized boulders, if available.
- Safe places during thunderstorms include cars and large buildings, the larger, the better.
- Do *not* seek shelter in a tent because its metal rods conduct electricity. For the same reason, do *not* wear a metal-frame backpack during a lightning storm.
- Keep away from puddles, streams, and other bodies of water, because water conducts electricity.
- Do *not* remain on or next to a horse. Sitting on a horse increases your height; standing next to a horse gives lightning a larger target.
- If you are retreating to safety during a storm, stay as low as possible, remove children from back carriers, and walk with your legs wide apart.
- If you are boating, return to shore immediately.

Be aware of the fickleness of mountain weather. Storms can approach extremely rapidly. If you see a storm, the most prudent course is to retreat at once to a safe area. Don't proceed to a summit if you hear or see signs of an electrical storm.

DRINKING WATER—GIARDIASIS PREVENTION

Always carry a large quantity of safe drinking water—at least one quart per person. It is *not* safe to drink from any of the lakes and streams in the parks. The waters may be infested with giardia, a parasite that wreaks havoc in the human digestive system. Giardia infestation is caused when mammals such as muskrats defecate in or near the water, or when water has been contaminated by the careless disposal of human waste. Symptoms of giardiasis include diarrhea, abdominal distention, gas, and cramps, appearing 7 to 10 days after infection. If you suffer these symptoms, it is necessary to obtain treatment from a physician.

To purify water, boil it for 3 to 6 minutes. You may also disinfect the water chemically or by filtration, but these methods have not been proven to be as effective as heat. All water that might be swallowed must be treated, including water used for cooking, cleaning dishes, and brushing teeth.

To help prevent the spread of giardiasis and other harmful diseases, dig temporary latrines at least 8 inches deep, 8 to 10 inches wide, and 200 feet away from water sources, trails, and campsites. After use, fill the hole with loose soil and tap down

The Tetons

lightly. Do not bury the paper; pack it out. Of course, campers should wash hands thoroughly after use of the latrine. Parents should teach children safe toileting practices to protect their health and to keep lakes, streams, and rivers clean.

TICKS

Ticks can transmit Lyme disease. The symptoms of Lyme disease in advanced cases are severe, including arthritis, meningitis, neurological problems, and cardiac symptoms. These symptoms can occur a few weeks to over a year after the tick bite. Early signs can include a rash around the infected tick bite and flu-like symptoms. Timely diagnosis and treatment can cure or lessen the severity of the disease. If you or your family experiences these symptoms after a tick bite, immediately contact your physician.

Although there have been very few tick-related illnesses reported in Yellowstone and Grand Teton national parks, it is prudent to take the following precautions:

- Use an insect repellent containing DEET or permethrin; spray on shoes and clothing, especially socks, pant legs, and cuffs, and shirt sleeves and cuffs.
- Avoid direct application of DEET to the skin, for this potentially harmful chemical is easily absorbed. DEET can also damage rayon, acetate, and spandex, but is safe on nylon, cotton, and wool. When buying DEET, choose a formula containing no more than 35 percent DEET. Tests have shown that this amount provides as much protection as formulas containing higher concentrations. In addition, there are several repellents formulated especially for children.
- Tuck pants into boots, and button cuffs and collars.
- Wear light-colored clothing to spot ticks more easily.
- Check frequently for ticks on skin, scalp, and clothing. This may be done on rest breaks while hiking. Ticks often spend many hours on a body before they transmit the virus, so there is no need to panic if you find a tick. Infection can, nevertheless, be transmitted soon after the tick attaches, so check regularly.
- Use caution when visiting prime tick habitats: grassy, brushy, low elevation areas (4,000 to 6,500 feet) from mid-March until mid-July.

If you should discover a tick, remove it using tweezers, pulling it straight out. It is important to remove all head and mouth parts to prevent infection. After removal, wash the area with soap and water. Even though ticks are rare in late summer and fall, you should still check your family regularly.

SNOWFIELDS, ICEFIELDS, STREAMS, AND WATERFALLS

Be extremely cautious when traveling over snow or ice. Snow and icefields may persist in both parks until late summer at higher elevations. Never venture near the edge of snow or ice slopes or cornices. These areas can be treacherous and unstable. If you are hiking at high altitudes, check with rangers for snow conditions. If you do venture into areas where snow remains, be prepared with the necessary gear, such as crampons, ropes, and ice axes.

Streams and rivers can also be dangerous. The current of even small streams can be strong, especially in spring and early summer and particularly for children. Take appropriate precautions when crossing streams. Take the time to walk up and downstream to find the safest place to ford. Hold hands or interlock arms when crossing, and undo the waist and chest straps of all packs. Never allow children to play unsupervised on stream banks. The frigid temperatures of snow- and groundwater-fed streams quickly disable even good swimmers.

The parks' waterfalls also present significant hazards. Slick rocks and steep drop-offs near waterfalls warrant an extra close watch on children.

FALLING TREES

The 1988 Yellowstone fires left many areas with standing dead trees. These trees may fall with little warning. In such areas, hike cautiously, be alert for falling trees, and don't stop to rest beneath a burned snag. If high winds develop, leave a burned area immediately, if possible.

LOST AND FOUND

The parks' trails are generally well-marked and easy to follow. In Yellowstone, at frequent intervals along each trail, the NPS has nailed square orange metal markers to trailside trees. As an extra precaution, always carry current topographic maps for the area in which you are hiking. Visitor centers and local outdoor supply stores sell a variety of maps, including United States Geological Survey (USGS) maps. These are particularly useful because they show terrain and elevation by means of contour lines. If you have old maps, make sure they are up to date. Finally, buy waterproof maps, or carry maps in a waterproof pouch.

Also, carry a reliable compass and know how to use it in conjunction with your topographic map. If you don't feel confident, check with outing clubs in your area for instruction. Good books providing instruction in compass use are also available (see appendix C).

Children are particularly vulnerable to getting lost and are less able to care for themselves if they do. When hiking or biking, do not let children stray from your sight. Take the following preventive measures to guard against potentially traumatic or dangerous situations:

- Teach children to stay with the group.
- Instruct children never to leave designated trails.
- Give children whistles, with strict instructions to use the whistles only when lost.
- Instruct children to remain in one place if they become lost. That way, they can be found more easily.
- If children must move while lost, teach them how to build "ducks" by placing a smaller stone on top of a larger stone. By leaving a trail of ducks, the children will more easily be found.

SIGN IN, PLEASE

In Yellowstone National Park, hikers should sign in at the trail register found at the beginning of each backcountry trail. In the event of an emergency, the date and time of your departure and your stated destination is critical information for park rangers.

RATTLESNAKES

The only poisonous snake inhabiting the parks is the prairie rattlesnake occasionally found in the northwest corner of Yellowstone, near Gardiner, Montana. The snake can reach 4 feet long and has dark splotches on a brownish background with a rattle on its tail. Although certainly poisonous, its poison is rarely fatal to adults. The prairie rattlesnake usually inhabits cliffs or rocky outcrops, but it is uncommon in Yellowstone. Report sightings to the nearest ranger station.

The snakes most likely to be seen in the two parks are the rubber boa (brown with a yellow belly), the wandering garter (brownish

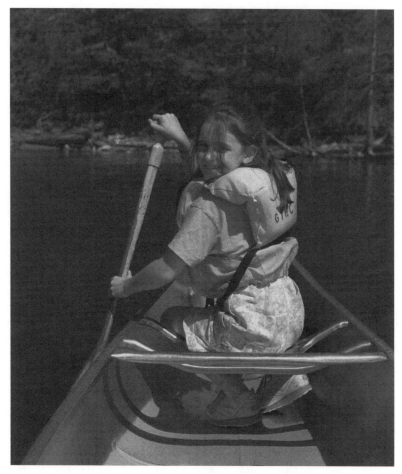

Canoeing on Jackson Lake, Grand Teton National Park

green with three longitudinal stripes), and the valley garter snake (bright yellow and red lateral stripes with dark head). All are harmless to humans and usually measure less than 2½ feet long.

FIRST-AID KIT

Carry a first-aid kit on *every* outing. Commercially packaged kits are available in convenient sizes. If you purchase one, check its contents against the following list and supplement if necessary.

To make your own first-aid kit, simply purchase the items listed below and place them in a nylon stuff bag, zippered container, or aluminum box.

- Adhesive bandage strips: Bring an abundant supply; their psychological value to children cannot be underestimated.
- Butterfly bandages for minor lacerations
- Sterile gauze pads (4 x 4 inches) for larger wounds
- Adhesive tape to attach dressings
- Antibiotic ointment to treat wounds and cuts
- Moleskin for blisters
- Triangle bandages for slings
- Athletic tape for multiple uses
- Children's pain reliever
- Adult pain reliever
- Betadine swabs (povidone iodine) for an antiseptic
- Alcohol pads to cleanse skin
- Elastic bandage for sprains
- Knife with scissors and tweezers: Tweezers are needed to remove ticks and splinters.
- Space blanket for emergency warmth
- First-aid instruction booklet

Checklist for Safe Hiking

THE TEN "PLUS" ESSENTIALS

Use the following checklist before departing on each of your outings. It includes the Ten Essentials compiled by The Mountaineers and adds a few extra essentials specific to the needs of children. Bringing the following items prepares you for emergencies.

1. Extra clothing. The extra weight ensures against cold, cranky children and hypothermia. A space blanket is also a useful and lightweight addition.
2. Extra food and water. Extra food is useful as a hiking incentive and essential in emergencies.
3. Sunglasses. Hats with visors offer protection for youngsters too young to wear sunglasses.
4. Knife. A knife has multiple uses in emergency situations.
5. Firestarter candle or chemical fuel. In an emergency, you may need to make a fire for warmth or for signaling.

6. First-aid kit. Indispensable, see preceding list.
7. Matches in a waterproof container. Containers are available at outdoor supply stores or use a 35 mm film canister.
8. Flashlight. A flashlight is needed to negotiate trails at night or to prepare a camp at unexpected hours.
9. Map. Carry a current map in a waterproof case.
10. Compass. Know how to use it.
11. Sunscreen. Test for skin sensitivity before the trip.
12. Whistles. These are to be used only in the event children become lost.
13. Water purification tablets. The tablets ensure a source of emergency drinking water.
14. Bike repair kit. A necessary item for bicyclists.
15. Bike helmets. One for each rider and passenger.
16. Personal flotation devices. One for each passenger.

A Note About Safety

Safety is an important concern in all outdoor activities. No guidebook can alert you to every hazard or anticipate the limitations of every reader. Therefore, the descriptions of roads, trails, routes, and natural features in this book are not representations that a particular place or excursion will be safe for your party. When you follow any of the routes described in this book, you assume responsibility for your own safety. Under normal conditions, such excursions require the usual attention to traffic, road and trail conditions, weather, terrain, the capabilities of your party, and other factors. Keeping informed on current conditions and exercising common sense are the keys to a safe, enjoyable outing.

The Mountaineers

CHAPTER

1

Yellowstone and Grand Teton National Parks:
An Overview

The Greater Yellowstone Ecosystem

Yellowstone National Park is the second largest national park in the continental United States. At nearly 3,500 square miles, it exceeds the size of Rhode Island and Delaware combined. Just to the south, Grand Teton National Park encompasses another 40 miles of alpine peaks. Together, the parks provide a tremendous amount of wilderness to explore.

Yet to understand these wild lands, it is necessary to grasp a still larger picture. Grand Teton and Yellowstone constitute the heart of the Greater Yellowstone Ecosystem (GYE), the largest relatively intact temperate ecosystem on earth. Within the borders of the GYE are two national parks, seven national forests, three national wildlife refuges, and over one million acres of privately owned land. The GYE is more than six times the size of Yellowstone itself.

The scope of the GYE is most easily grasped by imagining an

Opposite: Jumping for joy in the Tetons

aerial view of the Yellowstone region. From the air, the GYE is discernable as an island of green; a high, rolling, forested plateau bordered by spectacular mountains and surrounded by arid plains and basins. Described another way, the GYE encompasses the migration routes and winter ranges of the greater Yellowstone ungulates (elk, bison, deer, antelope, bighorn sheep), the reaches of Yellowstone's extensive geothermal system, and the watersheds of the three major rivers born in the mountains of Yellowstone.

What is the importance of the GYE? The very health of the parks' wildlife, rivers, and geothermal features depends on the protection of the greater ecosystem. In the area surrounding the GYE, development has fundamentally changed the land, so that little of the original flora and fauna remains. Within the GYE, however, most of the plants and animals found in pre-Columbian times still survive. The GYE is one of the last strongholds in the lower 48 for numerous species listed as threatened and endangered, including the grizzly bear, the peregrine falcon, the whooping crane, and the bald eagle.

Yet in 1988, the Wilderness Society identified Yellowstone as one of the country's most endangered national parks. Timber harvesting, oil and gas development, forest road building, hard rock mining, recreation development, and rural subdivisions endanger water quality, wildlife habitat, and scenic values. As you travel through the parks, you will hear and read much about the GYE. Hiking, biking, and paddling take you seamlessly from national park, to national forest, to private land, to national wildlife refuge. The realization that all these lands are integrally connected and equally worthy of protection is the essence of the GYE. The parks' wildlife, including its trout, grizzlies, eagles, and bison cannot survive on islands of preservation. Maintenance of the age-old ecosystem is the key to their survival, and it must be the goal of all who love this region.

Yellowstone National Park

In the summer of 1988, extraordinary drought conditions and gale force winds fueled ferocious fires in Yellowstone. Despite $120 million spent to stop the fires, six uncontrollable blazes swept through almost 50 percent of the park. Yet the fires' effect was not catastrophic. The fires burned in a mosaic pattern, taking patches of forest in some places but leaving adjacent acres untouched. Soil was sterilized in less than 1 percent of the forests burned. Almost half of the total 1.1 million acres burned endured only surface burn, in which only the understory was consumed. By the spring of 1989, dramatic rejuvenation had already begun. Green grasses and bright pink fireweed blanketed the fire-touched areas.

Yellowstone's wildlife escaped relatively unscathed. Less than 1 percent of the park's large animals were killed by the fires. In fact, bison and elk ignored the inferno, grazing as close as 50 yards to the burning forest. The fires also had positive effects. Post-fire plant growth today provides richer grazing and browsing for the park's ungulates. Birds, like woodpeckers and mountain bluebirds, are thriving, for burned snags provide homes and insects. In addition, the fires' removal of forest debris and creation of new meadows aid

Fly-fishing on Yellowstone Lake

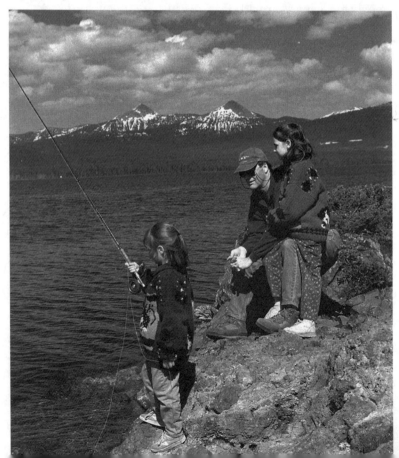

birds of prey, like eagles, hawks, and owls, and larger predators, such as grizzlies. In general, experts believe that plant and animal diversity will noticeably increase in the quarter century following the fire.

What about its impact on trails? The scenic value of much of the park has been affected, but try not to prejudge. Burned areas have a singular beauty, especially in late summer. The blackened trunks create striking silhouettes against the blue sky and contrast pleasingly with bright green grasses and vibrant flowers. The burns also expose panoramic vistas not seen in a century and greatly increase your chance of seeing wildlife.

Two-thirds of the earth's geothermal features are found in Yellowstone National Park. While the earth's molten rock layer (magma) normally lies 6 miles beneath the surface, in Yellowstone, the magma sits only 3 miles deep (in places, it's only 1 mile beneath the surface). This molten rock heats water from rain and snow that seeps through fissures in the sub-surface rock. The magma's heat turns the water to steam, and a build-up of pressure eventually brings it to the surface. The result is a wondrous collection of over ten thousand colorful hot springs, hissing fumaroles, roiling mud pots, and more than two hundred explosive geysers. Many are easily observed from boardwalks at the Upper, Middle, and Lower Geyser basins, at beautiful Norris Geyser Basin, at Mammoth Hot Springs, and on backcountry trails.

One of the most awesome but underrated sights in Yellowstone National Park is the Grand Canyon of the Yellowstone River. Its yellow, orange, and pink rock walls rise 1,200 vertical feet above the river's whitewater. Two magnificent waterfalls roar at its head. The larger of the two, the Lower Falls, stands almost three times as tall as Niagara Falls. Rock pinnacles on the canyon walls support osprey nests 5 feet in diameter. From the riverbanks clouds of steam rise from thermal activity beneath the canyon floors. This fascinating place can be experienced from a variety of vantage points and trails.

Yellowstone has been called America's Serengeti for its tens of thousands of highly visible elk, bison, antelope, moose, and deer. Although bears no longer beg along the roads, hundreds of grizzlies and black bears roam the backcountry. Since their historic reintroduction in 1995, wolves also make up a small but thriving population in Yellowstone! Nowhere else in the continental United States is wildlife so awesome and visible.

Grand Teton National Park

Author-naturalist Gary Ferguson wrote that the Tetons "are to mountains what the Grand Canyon is to gorges; what Chartres is to cathedrals; what dark chocolate is to desserts." Ferguson aptly describes the awesome sweep of glistening rock rising 7,000 feet from the valley floor in a singular, magnificent gesture, wholly without foothills. This triumphant uplift is the result of a fault block, wherein enormous rock masses rose and slipped along a fault line on the eastern base of the Teton Range.

The movement of glaciers over the course of 200,000 years sculpted the Teton peaks into the jagged mountains we admire today. During the last Ice Age, approximately 10,000 years ago, immense tongues of ice, thousands of feet high, slid from its peaks, tearing knife-edge ridges and grinding U-shaped canyons. The glaciers pushed thousands of tons of debris down to the base of the range. When the glaciers melted, lakes were created at the foot of the mountains. These lakes reflect in heartbreaking perfection the chiseled peaks towering above them. Glaciers still hang high above the valley. The scene is postcard-perfect.

In the brief Teton summer, magnificent gardens of wildflowers grace the valley, mountainsides, and alpine meadows of the park. Hikers find fields of lavender lupine and rock gardens graced with electric-blue alpine forget-me-nots. Glorious flowers are a fine reward for hiking the park's steep trails.

Planning Your Trip

PREPLANNING IS ESSENTIAL

Because of the overwhelming number of park visitors each summer (over 4 million), it is necessary to make camping and lodging reservations as early as possible. It is not unusual to make reservations one year in advance. For lodging in Grand Teton and Yellowstone, it is best to firm up your plans at least 6 months prior to arrival. Reservations are also accepted for popular activities such as horseback riding and western cook-outs.

Backpackers must plan ahead also. Grand Teton National Park accepts requests (free-of-charge) for summer backcountry campsites from January through May. For particularly accessible and attractive sites, backpackers must get their requests in early.

Mount Moran above Colter Bay

Backpackers in Yellowstone may reserve campsites beginning on April 1 for that calendar year.

To plan your visit, read the following sections and decide when, how, and where you want to go. For the most complete and up-to-date information on both parks, consult their websites at www.nps.gov/yell (YNP) and www.nps.gov/grte (GTNP). You can also write or call both parks to request maps and information. Contact the park concessionaires for information on lodging and activities. Request information from outfitters if you're interested in specialty trips such as kayaking or horseback-riding overnights. Call for catalogs about organized backpacking trips, nature classes, or children's science camps. If you're planning to fly, contact airlines early to secure the dates you want. Flights are especially limited to Jackson, so reservations must be made far in advance.

If all this planning is distasteful, it is, of course, still possible to arrive at a park entrance gate with only a packed car and an open mind. Several good campgrounds are still first come, first served, and there are often cancellations at park lodging. This approach can work if you have lots of time to explore the region and are highly flexible. My recommendation, however, is plan at least part of your stay so that you will not be shut out of an area you really want to see.

Important Contact Information

Yellowstone National Park Visitor Information
(307) 344-7381; www.nps.gov/yell
Yellowstone Lodging and Activities Information
(307) 344-7311
Grand Teton National Park Visitor Information
(307) 739-3600; www.nps.gov/grte
Grand Teton Lodging and Activities Information
(307) 543-2811
Grand Teton Campground Information
(307) 739-3603

HOW TO GET THERE

By car: Yellowstone National Park has five entrances. The North Entrance is reached via U.S. 89 from Gardiner, MT (165 miles from Billings and 79 miles from Bozeman, MT); the Northeast Entrance is reached via U.S. 212 from Silver Gate and Cooke City (127 miles from Billings, MT, 68 miles from Cody, WY); the East Entrance is accessed via U.S. 14–16–20 (53 miles from Cody, WY); the South Entrance is reached via U.S. 89–191–287 from Flagg Ranch, WY (56 miles from Jackson, WY); and the West Entrance is reached via U.S. 20 from West Yellowstone, MT (90 miles from Bozeman, MT). In winter, only the North Entrance is open to automobile use. Because of snow, the other four entrances are closed to automobile traffic from October 31 to May 1.

Grand Teton National Park can be reached from the north by traveling south 8 miles on U.S. 89–191–287 from Yellowstone's South Entrance. Its East Entrance at Moran Junction is reached by driving west approximately 60 miles on U.S. 26/287 from Dubois, WY. Its South Entrance at Moose Junction (Park Headquarters) is reached by driving north 12 miles from Jackson, WY on U.S. 89–191–287.

By air: If your initial destination is Yellowstone National Park, daily air service is available to the following cities: Bozeman, MT (79 miles from the North Entrance); Billings, MT (127 miles from the Northeast Entrance); and Cody, WY (53 miles from the East

Entrance). Limited summer air service is also available to West Yellowstone, MT, just outside the West Entrance. If your destination is Grand Teton National Park, daily air service is available to Jackson Hole Airport, located within Grand Teton National Park, 10 miles north of the town of Jackson, WY. Service is also available to Idaho Falls on the west slope of the Tetons, about 100 miles from Grand Teton's Park Headquarters in Moose, WY.

By bus: Greyhound Lines service Bozeman, Livingston, and West Yellowstone, MT. From these cities, Karst Stage offers connecting service to Yellowstone's North and West entrances. Powder River Transportation offers service to the East Entrance from Cody, WY. Gray Line Tours services Yellowstone's South Entrance and Grand Teton National Park from Jackson, WY, (307) 733-4325. Yellowstone Park Co. also services Livingston and Cooke City, MT, and Grand Teton National Park. AmFac Parks and Resorts offers bus tours of Yellowstone National Park from locations within the park, (307) 344-7311. Buffalo Bus Lines offers tours from West Yellowstone, (800) 742-0665.

Rental cars: Rental cars are available at airports and in major towns near both parks.

WHEN TO GO

Spring (May through June): Spring visitors experience cool, sometimes cold, wet, and always unpredictable weather. Although the weather may be less than ideal, spring is a time to experience the parks' beauty in relative solitude. Runoff dramatically swells rivers and waterfalls. In June at lower elevations, flowers bloom gloriously. Wildlife viewing is prime: large mammals are still in the valleys, migratory birds are just returning, bears are foraging, and mule deer, elk, pronghorn, and bison are bearing their young.

Because of persistent snow and/or soggy trails, spring hiking is generally limited to trails at lower elevations. Winter conditions prevail above 6,500 feet through May and persist above 8,500 feet through June. Daytime temperatures average in the 50s to 60s at lower elevations, with nighttime lows in the 30s. Campers should not be surprised to see a dusting of snow on the ground and frost on their cars in the morning. Periods of heavy rain are likely.

Summer (July through August): This is the tourist season, and visitors must be prepared to share the parks' treasures. Hiking begins in earnest, along with peak mosquito season. Elk and moose retreat to forests and higher ground to escape the heat, bugs, and tourists. A profusion of flowers graces the meadows.

In July, daytime high temperatures reach the 70s, although nights are still cold (15 to 40 degrees F) especially at higher elevations. Daytime temperatures in the valleys and in Jackson may climb into the 80s on sunny summer days. Mornings are often brilliant, with clear, bright blue skies. While thunderstorms threaten most afternoons, the sky generally clears after an hour or so. In early July, meadows and trails may still be wet.

In August, hiking is prime. The biting bugs retreat noticeably. Days are warm (65 to 80 degrees F), and nights are comfortably brisk, though sometimes cold (25 to 40 degrees F). Afternoon thunderstorms persist. Trails are drier in August than in July and are usually free of snow. Wildflowers bloom in alpine areas, and berries ripen throughout the parks.

It is important to remember that cold, wet weather can persist into July and August. While some park summers are dry and sunny, in other years, "summer" fails to arrive. The rule is to be prepared for severe conditions in any season.

Fall (September through October): Early autumn is exquisite, with excellent hiking conditions. Summer crowds are gone, and wildlife viewing peaks. Large animals return en masse to the valleys. Elk are in their splendor performing their fascinating mating rituals. Ducks and geese fill the ponds. Aspen flash their gold, particularly in the Tetons. Days are often crisp and bright (40 to 45 degrees F), but noticeably shorter and cooler. Nights are cold (15 to 35 degrees in September, 0 to 35 degrees in October). Heavy snows are possible beginning in September, but more likely in October. Rain is common in both months.

WHERE TO STAY
Park Lodging

There are many advantages to staying within the parks. Driving time is reduced and park programs, campfire talks, and ranger-led hikes are easily attended. Wildlife viewing is more fruitful, since dawn and dusk are the most rewarding viewing times. Park sunrises and sunsets are spectacular, whether on Jackson Lake, atop Signal Mountain, on the rim of the Grand Canyon, or on magnificent Yellowstone Lake.

Within the parks, accommodations of all kinds are available, from suites at historic inns to bare-bones tent shelters. Cabins may be rented at several locations. Cabins offer a rustic, historic, inexpensive, and yet comfortable experience for noncamping families and are especially enjoyed by children. Both Roosevelt Lodge Cabins in Yellowstone and Colter Bay Cabins in Grand Teton are located in particularly fine settings.

YELLOWSTONE NATIONAL PARK

Yellowstone accommodations run the gamut from elegant to rustic. Consider your needs, pocketbook, and locational preference. For all accommodations, it is necessary to reserve well in advance by contacting Xanterra Parks and Resorts, Yellowstone National Park, WY 82190, (307) 344-7311, or www.travelyellowstone.com.

Lodging is available at all locations from mid-June until Labor Day. In spring and fall, the selection is more limited. In winter, only the Mammoth Hot Springs Hotel and Old Faithful Snow Lodge are open.

North Yellowstone

- *Mammoth Hot Springs Hotel and Cabins:* Modern hotel and cabins located at very busy Mammoth Hot Springs near Park Headquarters, Albright Visitor Center, and numerous stores and restaurants. Corral and guided trail rides nearby. NPS programs at Albright Visitor Center and Mammoth Campground as well as at Tower Campground, 18 miles to the east.
- *Roosevelt Lodge Cabins:* Rustic cabins (wood-burning stoves, no bath) located in quiet, historic setting near Tower Fall and the Lamar Valley. Small store and dining room. Corral with guided trail and stagecoach rides. NPS programs at nearby Tower and Mammoth campgrounds. Excellent choice in spring and early summer when snow persists at higher elevations. Opportunities for observing wildlife (including wolves) are superb in the beautiful Lamar Valley.

Central Yellowstone

- *Canyon Lodge and Cabins:* Modern lodge and cabins located at scenic north rim of the Grand Canyon of the Yellowstone. Busy and congested complex includes stores, cafeteria, restaurants, post office, and Canyon Visitor Center. Located near wildlife-filled Hayden Valley. Corral with guided trail rides nearby. NPS programs at adjacent Canyon Campground and visitor center. Twelve miles from Norris Geyser Basin. Excellent hiking trails nearby.

South Yellowstone

- *Lake Yellowstone Hotel and Cabins and Lake Lodge Cabins:* Located on the scenic shore of Yellowstone Lake. Choose from elegant, historic Lake Yellowstone Hotel or rustic cabins adjacent to the hotel and lodge. Hotel offers formal dining room and snack bar; lodge provides a cafeteria. Near stores and visitor center at Fishing Bridge. Boat rentals and tours at nearby Bridge Bay Marina. NPS programs at Fishing Bridge Visitor Center and Bridge Bay Campground. Good fishing and superb hiking trails nearby.
- *Grant Village Motel:* Modern motel located on Yellowstone Lake. Sprawling complex includes Grant Village Visitor Center, stores, and restaurants. NPS programs at adjacent Grant Village Campground. Near West Thumb Geyser Basin. Good fishing nearby.
- *Old Faithful Inn, Old Faithful Lodge Cabins, and Old Faithful Snow Lodge:* Very busy complex located at Old Faithful (Upper Geyser Basin) includes Old Faithful Visitor Center, numerous stores, restaurants, and cafeteria. Accommodations range from the impressive, historic Old Faithful Inn to the Snow Lodge (renovated in 1999) and cabins. Area is very congested in summer. NPS programs at Old Faithful Visitor Center and Madison Campground (16 miles north). Near Midway and Lower Geyser basins and Firehole Canyon Drive swimming hole.

Grand Teton National Park

Grand Teton National Park also hosts a wide variety of accommodations. Beginning at the northern tip of the park just south of Yellowstone's South Entrance, find the newly constructed Flagg Ranch Resort offering lodge rooms, cabins, and a corral, open June to mid-October. Situated on the Snake River north of Jackson Lake, Flagg Ranch lacks the alpine scenery and proximity to excellent hiking that other locations offer. NPS programs are held at the Flagg Ranch Campground. For reservations call (800) 443-2311.

For more classic Teton scenery, try beautiful Colter Bay located about 15 miles south of Flagg Ranch. Directly across Jackson Lake from magnificent Mount Moran, find the well-appointed Colter Bay Cabins near a marina, corral, and fine hiking trails. Cabins are open mid-May to late September. More rustic are the Colter Bay Tent Cabins, open early June to early September. These canvas-sided "cabins" have bunk beds, wood stoves, grills, and picnic tables. NPS programs are held at the adjacent Colter Bay Campground and Visitor Center as well as at the Indian Arts Museum. A few miles south, Jackson Lake Lodge offers top motel accommodations with swimming pool, scenic views, good wildlife viewing, and restaurants, open late May to early October. Find NPS programs at nearby Colter Bay. Those staying at the Colter Bay Cabins and Tent Cabins also have use of the swimming pool at Jackson Lake Lodge. For reservations for all of the above, contact the Grand Teton Lodge Company, Grand Teton National Park, P.O. Box 240, Moran, WY 83013, (800) 628-9988 or (307) 543-2855.

Signal Mountain Lodge is scenically located just south of Jackson Lake Lodge on Jackson Lake, about 15 miles north of park headquarters in Moose. The lodge offers motel accommodations, a restaurant, and marina. NPS programs are held at the adjacent Signal Mountain Campground. Contact Signal Mountain Lodge at P.O. Box 50, Moran, WY, (307) 543-2831. Further south, in an exclusive setting near world-renowned Jenny Lake, the Jenny Lake Lodge offers rustic elegance in elaborate cabins with formal dining, as well as a private corral. Open late May to early October. NPS programs at nearby Jenny Lake Campground. Call 1-800-628-9988 for reservations. Lastly, just steps from Park Headquarters in Moose and a short drive away from superb trails, find Dornan's Spur Ranch Cabins set along the Snake River, near a small cluster of stores and restaurants, open year-round. NPS programs at Moose Visitor Center and nearby Jenny Lake Campground. Call (307) 733-2522 for information.

Campgrounds
YELLOWSTONE NATIONAL PARK
There are twelve campgrounds in Yellowstone National Park, ranging from the gargantuan (420 sites) to the relatively intimate (29 sites). Advance reservations may be made at the five campgrounds (Bridge Bay, Canyon, Grant Village, Madison and Fishing Bridge RV Park) operated by Xanterra Parks and Resorts. To make reservations, call (307) 344-7311; write Xanterra Parks and Resorts, P.O. Box 165, Yellowstone National Park, WY 82190; or go online at www.travelyellowstone.com/camping. Same-day reservations can be made by calling the above number or by checking at a campground registration desk. All other campgrounds are

operated by the NPS on a first-come, first-served basis. For these campgrounds, it is necessary to arrive as early as possible on the day you plan to camp. In July and August, many campgrounds are filled to capacity by mid-morning. Between June 15 and September 15, camping is limited to a maximum of 14 days at all campgrounds.

For information about NPS campgrounds, call (307) 344-7381 or write NPS, Visitor Services Office, Yellowstone National Park, WY 82190. Yellowstone campgrounds are indicated on the park map at the beginning of this book and are described in the chart on the next page:

Campfire, Yellowstone National Park

Campground	Number of sites	Open	Toilet	Showers/Laundry Nearby	Dump Station	Comments
North Yellowstone						
Mammoth*	85	Year-round	Flush	No	No	Open setting, little privacy
Indian Creek*	75	Early June–mid-Sept.	Pit	No	No	Some nice sites near river
Pebble Creek*	32	Mid-June–early Sept.	Pit	No	No	Near Northeast Entrance
Slough Creek*	29	Late May–late Oct.	Pit	No	No	Pretty creekside setting
Tower Fall*	32	Late May–mid-Sept.	Pit	No	No	Limited privacy
Central Yellowstone						
Norris*	116	Mid-May–mid-Sept.	Flush	No	No	Pretty sites near Gibbon River
Canyon Village**	272	Early June–early Sept.	Flush	Yes	Yes	Forest setting
Bridge Bay**	430	Late May–late Sept.	Flush	Yes	Yes	Very congested, little privacy
Fishing Bridge RV**	344	Mid-May–mid-Sept.	Flush	Yes	Sewer hook-ups	Hard-sided campers only
Madison**	280	Early May–late Oct.	Flush	No	No	Little privacy
South Yellowstone						
Grant Village**	425	Late June–mid-Oct.	Flush	Yes	Yes	Huge campground on Yellowstone Lake
Lewis Lake*	85	Mid-June–late Oct.	Pit	No	No	Forested site on Lewis Lake

* First come/first served

** Reserve through AmFac Parks and Resorts, (307) 344-7311

GRAND TETON NATIONAL PARK

Five NPS campgrounds are located in Grand Teton National Park. All are operated on a first-come, first-served basis; reservations are not accepted. In Grand Teton, it is imperative to arrive as early as possible at the campground of your choice. At Jenny Lake Campground in August, for example, all available sites are assigned *before* 8:00 A.M. To avoid disappointment, check at entrance stations and visitor centers for current status of campgrounds and approximate filling times. See the park map at the beginning of this book.

Campgrounds are located in the following areas: *Lizard Creek* open mid-June to early September, 60 sites; *Colter Bay* open late May to late September, 310 sites, marina, corral, restaurant, museum, visitor center, scenic location near hiking trails; *Signal*

Mountain open early May to mid-October, 86 sites, marina, restaurant, store, ranger station, located on Jackson Lake; *Jenny Lake* open late May to late September, 49 sites, tents only, near store and ranger station, scenic location near hiking trails; *Gros Ventre* open early May to early October, 360 sites.

Backpacking

Both Yellowstone and Grand Teton national parks have designated campsite systems to prevent overuse of the backcountry. A permit is required for all overnight trips. For Yellowstone outings, permits must be obtained at a ranger station no more than 48 hours before the camping date. Advance reservations for some backcountry campsites may be made in writing or in person for a $20 fee. To obtain the necessary forms, write the Backcountry Office, P.O. Box 168, YNP, WY 82190; use the Online Backcountry Trip Planner at www.nps.gov/yell; or inquire at a ranger station. The maximum stay per campsite varies from 1 to 3 nights per trip. Only a portion of backcountry campsites will be available for advance reservations. Thus, you may choose to wait until you arrive in the park to reserve your site and obtain your permit. Questions may be directed to the backcountry office at (307) 344-2160.

For backcountry overnights in Grand Teton, obtain a permit at the Moose or Colter Bay visitor centers or the Jenny Lake Ranger Station. Your length of stay is restricted based upon the specific campsite. Backcountry campsites may also be reserved by mail or fax between January 1 and May 15 for a $15 fee by writing to Grand Teton National Park, P.O. Drawer 170, Moose, WY 83012 or faxing (307) 739-3438. To obtain a reservation, submit your itinerary, including dates, camping zone selection for each night, and the number of people in your party. Include a second choice itinerary in case a campsite is filled. For help in preparing this request, call the Permit Office at (307) 739-3309. Reservations are also accepted by fax at (307) 739-3438. There are several backcountry campsites in both parks just a few miles from park trailheads that present ideal family backpacking opportunities. These campsites are noted in the trail descriptions and are also highlighted in the Trip Finder for easy reference (appendix A).

Backpacking in the GYE calls for extra precautions to prevent bear encounters. Backpackers should follow the safety measures set out in the Introduction. In addition, to protect your family, the bears, and the Yellowstone ecosystem, follow the guidelines on page 19.

Nearby Accommodations

A wide variety of lodging is available in the towns surrounding the parks. For information, contact the Chambers of Commerce in the following towns: West Yellowstone, MT, (406) 646-7701; Cooke City–Silver Gate, MT, (406) 838-2265; Gardiner, MT, (406) 848-7971; Cody, WY, (307) 587-2297; and Dubois, WY, (307) 455-2556. For information on lodging in Jackson, WY, call the Jackson Chamber of Commerce, (307) 733-3316, or Jackson Hole Central Reservations at (800) 443-6931 or (307) 733-4005, or write P.O. Box 2618, Jackson, WY 83001.

EMERGENCY MEDICAL SERVICES

For medical emergencies in either park, dial 911. To see a medical professional within the parks, consult the following:

In Yellowstone National Park, Yellowstone Park Medical Services (YPMS) provides health and emergency care at three park locations. YPMS's Lake Clinic, Pharmacy, and Hospital offers outpatient services, a full-service hospital, 24-hour ambulance, and emergency care. Lake Clinic is located near the Lake Yellowstone Hotel and is open daily, 8:30 A.M. to 8:30 P.M., (307) 242-7242. YPMS also operates clinics at Old Faithful, (307) 545-7325, open daily from 8:30 A.M. to 5:00 P.M., and at Mammoth Hot Springs, (307) 344-7965, open Monday through Friday only. In Grand Teton National Park, find the Grand Teton Medical Clinic, (307) 543-2514, near Jackson Lake Lodge. The clinic is open daily, 10:00 A.M. to 6:00 P.M. A full-service hospital, St. John's Hospital, is located in Jackson, WY, at 625 East Broadway, (307) 733-3636.

ACTIVITIES WITHIN THE PARKS AND NEARBY

Interpretive Programs

From Memorial Day through September, NPS ranger-naturalists run a fine program of guided walks, slide shows, museum tours, art classes, and even canoe trips. Most are offered free of charge and many are geared for children. For information, inquire at any visitor center. At Grand Teton, many of the park programs are listed in the free park newspaper, *Teewinot*. Both parks also offer junior ranger programs, a recommended activity for children over age seven. Inquire at a visitor center for more information.

Yellowstone National Park Visitor Centers and Museums

Yellowstone offers five visitor centers, located near lodging and major campgrounds, where rangers dispense information on trail conditions, camping, and interpretive programs. Many centers also contain informational exhibits. In addition, at each location the Yellowstone Association sells an extensive array of maps, trail guides, and natural history books. The centers are also the nucleus for many ranger-led programs and guided walks. In addition to visitor centers, Yellowstone operates two museums and two information stations. In spring and fall, check for hours of operation. Admission is free to all visitor centers and museums.

Albright (Mammoth) Visitor Center at Mammoth Hot Springs provides exhibits on the natural and human history of the park. Visitors may also view a short film. Open daily, year round, (307) 344-2263.

Canyon Visitor Center at Canyon Village hosts an extensive interpretive exhibit on the park's bison. Open daily, mid-May through Labor Day, (307) 242-2550.

Fishing Bridge Visitor Center houses an exhibit on the ecology of the lake region, including specimens of many Yellowstone birds. Open daily, mid-May through Labor Day, (307) 242-2450.

Grant Village Visitor Center provides exhibits on the 1988 fires and a short film, continuously shown. Open daily, mid-May through Labor Day, (307) 242-2650.

Old Faithful Visitor Center offers a short film on geothermal features and up-to-date information on geyser eruptions. Open daily, mid-April to October 31 and mid-December to mid-March, (307) 545-2750.

Norris Geyser Basin Museum provides exhibits on geothermal features. Open daily, mid-May through Labor Day, (307) 344-2812.

Museum of the National Park Ranger offers historical exhibits on the role and importance of park rangers. Located in the historic Norris Soldier Station, 21 miles south of Mammoth Hot Springs. Open daily, mid-May through Labor Day.

Madison Information Station is housed in a charming log cottage on the Madison River. Offers information and publications. Open daily, late May through Labor Day, (307) 344-2265.

Fishing Bridge Visitor Center, Yellowstone National Park

West Thumb Information Station offers publications and information. Open daily, late May through Labor Day.

Grand Teton National Park Visitor Centers and Museum

Colter Bay Visitor Center and Indian Arts Museum houses an impressive collection of Indian artifacts, including shields, pipes, weapons, ceremonial and domestic items, and a tepee. The museum sponsors ranger-led tours and craft demonstrations. The visitor center sells a wide range of publications, posters, maps, and cards. Nature films are shown continuously. Ranger-led hikes and junior naturalist programs meet at the center. Open daily, late May to October, (307) 739-3594.

Moose Visitor Center offers an outstanding collection of maps and nature books for children and adults, as well as topographic and natural history displays. The center is also a meeting place for the park's junior naturalist program. Open daily, year round, (307) 739-3399.

Flagg Ranch Information Station, 2.5 miles south of the Yellowstone boundary, offers books, maps, park information, as well as exhibits on J.D. Rockefeller, Jr., and the Greater Yellowstone area. Open daily, winter and summer.

Jenny Lake Visitor Center provides information on backcountry trips, hiking trails, and park interpretive programs. Also offers books and maps. Open daily, June to early September. (307) 739-3343.

Menor's Ferry Historic Site offers a cable ferry across the Snake River. Original ferry buildings house a collection of authentic implements and wagons used by homesteaders and an old-fashioned general store, now selling an assortment of "penny" candy. NPS brochure offers self-guided tour. Located just north of the Moose Entrance Station off Teton Park Road. Open daily in summer.

Cunningham Cabin Historic Site includes a partially restored cabin circa 1890. A NPS brochure provides a self-guided tour. Located off U.S. 89, about 5.5 miles south of Moran Junction. Open daily.

Nearby Museums

Jackson Hole Museum contains small but rich exhibits of the Native-American, fur-trade and early-settler eras of Jackson Hole. The museum is located at the corner of Glenwood and Deloney in downtown Jackson behind the historic Wort Hotel. Open daily, Memorial Day through September, (307) 733-2414. Admission fee.

National Wildlife Art Museum offers an extensive collection of wildlife paintings, sculptures, and photographs, including a special hands-on gallery for children. The museum also offers children's programs, studio classes, and performances. Located on U.S. 89 directly across from the National Elk Refuge. Open daily in summer, closed Mondays, October through May, (307) 733-5771. Admission fee.

National Fish Hatchery invites visitors to view the hatchery

and learn about native trout. Located off U.S. 89, just west of
the National Elk Refuge, 1 mile north of the town of Jackson.
Open daily, 8 A.M. to 4 P.M. Free admission.

Museum of the Yellowstone provides fine exhibits of native
animals, Indian artifacts, and relics of the region's early
settlement. Its theater shows a variety of nature and historical videos. Also offers an impressive bookstore. Located in
West Yellowstone, MT, at the Union Pacific Depot, just west
of the park entrance. Open daily, May through October, (406)
646-7814. Admission fee.

Grizzly Discovery Center contains a small museum on bears
and five live grizzlies which can be viewed in a small enclo-
sure. Located in Grizzly Park, adjacent to the park entrance
in West Yellowstone, MT. Open daily, year round, (406) 646-
7001 and (800) 257-2570. Admission fee.

The Snake River at Schwabachen's Landing

Nature Courses and Camps

The Yellowstone Institute offers year-round programs for children and adults on wildlife, history, culture, and the natural wonders of Yellowstone. Courses range from 1-day children's programs to 5-day backcountry pack trips. The offerings are impressive, and almost all involve hands-on field participation. For a catalog, contact the Yellowstone Institute, P.O. Box 117, Yellowstone National Park, WY 82190, (307) 344-2294.

Located just outside Grand Teton National Park, the Teton Science School offers a wide variety of high-quality field programs for children and adults. Programs for young students include residential courses offered year-round and summer day-camps. Contact the Teton Science School, P.O. Box 68, Kelly, WY 83011, (307) 733-4765, www.tetonscience.org.

Horseback Riding

Yellowstone and Grand Teton National Parks

Concessionaires in both parks offer trail rides. To ride, children must be 8 years of age, at least 4 feet tall, and accompanied by an adult. In Yellowstone, three corrals (Mammoth, Roosevelt, and Canyon) offer 1- and 2-hour rides. For those with younger children, there are stagecoach rides or rides in a horsedrawn wagon to a western cookout from Roosevelt Lodge. During the summer, reservations are required. Call Xanterra Parks and Resorts, (307) 344-7311. In Grand Teton National Park, take a 1-, 2-, 3-hour, or a half-day trail ride from corrals at Jackson Lake or Colter Bay Village. Horsedrawn wagon rides are also available. Those staying at Jenny Lake Lodge can use the corral at Jenny Lake. For reservations, call (800) 628-9988 or (307) 543-2855.

Outside the Park

Numerous ranches outside the park offer family trail rides. For inexperienced children, Spring Creek Ranch has gentle horses and an attentive staff. The ranch is scenically located just south of Jackson. For reservations, call W.W. Guides, (307) 733-8833. Other outfitters in the Jackson area offering trail rides include: Bar T-5 Corral, (307) 733-3534; Jackson Hole Trail Rides at Teton Village, (307) 733-6992; A/OK Corral near Hoback Junction, (307) 733-6556; Teton Crest Outfitter near Victor, ID, (208) 787-2968; Mill Iron Ranch (2- to 4-hour rides), (307) 733-6390; Bud Nelson

Outfitters, (307) 733-2843; and Grand Targhee Resort, on the west slope of the Tetons, (800) 827-4433.

For unparalleled adventure and superb scenery, try a backcountry pack trip just outside Grand Teton National Park. The Teton Crest Outfitter, P.O. Box 711, Wilson, WY 83014, (208) 787-2968 or 787-2924, tailors backcountry pack trips to suit family needs and abilities, with special attention to novice and child riders.

Rafting

Rafting the Snake River is an exciting and unforgettable family experience. Choose between a slow, scenic float trip or a wild whitewater excursion. If you opt for a scenic float, take the shorter, 5-mile trip when traveling with youngsters. Book your float trip for early morning or dusk for the greatest likelihood of seeing wildlife.

Children ages 6 and up are likely to prefer whitewater rafting. Rafting the rapids is like riding a roller coaster; the waves keep children wet, screaming, and thrilled. For maximum excitement, request a paddle boat (as opposed to an oar boat, in which only the guide controls the raft). Prior to booking your trip, ask about conditions and appropriateness for children. Early in the season, when the water is high, the river may be too scary and/or dangerous.

For whitewater rafting trips, contact Sands Wildwater River Trips (expert guides, children welcome, "U-paddle" rafts, scenic/whitewater combo available also), (307) 733-4410 or (800) 358-8184; O.A.R.S., Inc. (2- and 5-day rafting trips, minimum age 4 years), (800) 345-6277; Jackson Hole Whitewater (307) 733-1007 or (800) 648-2602; Dave Hansen Whitewater, (307) 733-6295; Lone Eagle Whitewater, (307) 733-1090 or (800) 321-3800; Mad River Boat Trips, (children must be over 6 years old), (307) 733-6203 or (800) 458-7238; Lewis and Clark Expeditions, (307) 733-4022 or (800) 824-5375; Barker–Ewing River Trips, (307) 733-1000 or (800) 448-4202; Mill Iron Ranch Rafting/Fishing Trips (not recommended for children under 5 years), (307) 733-6390.

The following outfitters offer scenic float trips: Barker–Ewing Scenic Tours, (307) 733-1800 or (800) 365-1800; Grand Teton Lodge Company (10-mile float only, no children under 6), (307) 543-2811; Triangle X Float Trips (children must be 4 years old), (307) 733-5500; National Park Float Trips (10-mile float only, children must be 4 years old), (307) 733-6445; Lewis and Clark Expeditions

(12-mile float or scenic/whitewater combo), (307) 733-4022 or (800) 824-5375.

Boating

In Yellowstone, boaters must obtain a boating permit for all boats. Permits can be purchased at all ranger stations and visitor centers. The park allows motorboats, canoes, rowboats, kayaks, and sailboats on Yellowstone and Lewis lakes. On Shoshone Lake, only oar-powered boats are permitted. All other lakes and rivers in Yellowstone are closed to boating. While boating, watch weather conditions carefully and exercise great caution due to the extremely cold water. Human survival time is measured in minutes in Yellowstone Lake. For rentals on Yellowstone Lake, go to Bridge Bay Marina (rowboats and motorboats). Bridge Bay Marina also offers scenic cruises and guided fishing trips. For information, call (307) 344-7311.

In Grand Teton, all privately owned vessels must also be registered. During the summer, purchase permits at the Moose and Colter Bay visitor centers and at the Signal Mountain, Buffalo, and John D. Rockefeller Memorial Parkway ranger stations. Motorized vessels are only allowed on Jackson, Jenny, and Phelps lakes.

For boat rentals in Grand Teton, contact Signal Mountain Lodge (canoes and motorized boats), (307) 543-2831; Colter Bay Marina (canoes, rowboats, and motorboats), no advance reservations, (307) 543-2811; and Teton Boating Company, Inc. at Jenny Lake (motorboats), (307) 733-2703. Outside the park, call Leisure Sports of Jackson (rafts, canoes, touring, and inflatable kayaks), (307) 733-3040; and Dornan's in Moose, WY (canoes and kayaks), (307) 733-2522.

Guided Kayaking and Canoeing Trips

Paddling is one of the best ways for families to enjoy the spectacular lakes of Yellowstone and Grand Teton national parks. To reach the backcountry and scenic waters of Yellowstone Lake, contact Far and Away Adventures, (208) 726-8888 or (800) 232-8588. Families are welcome, and both children and adults are taught kayaking and fly fishing in a remote and beautiful setting. For an unforgettable overnight trip on Jackson Lake, including kayak instruction, guided tours, and moonlight paddling, contact O.A.R.S., Inc. (1- to 3-day family trips), (209) 736-4677 or (800) 345-6277. Inflatable kayaks and two-person sea kayaks offer sufficient stability, even for novices and children. For paddling instruction and Snake River excursions, call the Snake River Kayak and Canoe School in Jackson, (307) 733-3127 or (800) 529-2501.

Fishing

Trout fishing is spectacular in the unspoiled waters of the GYE. Anglers in great numbers are lured to the parks by rainbow, brown, brook, and lake (Mackinaw) trout; Arctic grayling; and mountain whitefish. The GYE also supports one of the last wild inland populations of cutthroat trout.

Before fishing in either park, obtain a copy of the fishing regulations at a visitor center or ranger station and check for location-specific restrictions. These may include restrictive use of bait, catch-and-release only areas, limits on number and size of catch, and area closures. Waterways may be closed to protect sensitive nesting birds and threatened and endangered species, or to provide scenic viewing areas.

In all waterways, the NPS encourages catch-and-release fishing to preserve fish populations. This is accomplished by fly fishing with barbless hooks. Bait fishing is discouraged or prohibited, since studies show that a fish caught by bait and released has only a 52 percent survival rate. Release of fish hooked on lures and flies boasts a survival rate of 96 percent.

Yellowstone National Park operates a park-specific permit system for all anglers. Anglers 16 years of age and older must purchase a Special Use Permit. Anglers 12 to 15 years of age must obtain a nonfee permit. Children 11 and under may fish without a permit. Obtain permits at any ranger station or visitor center or at sporting goods stores in nearby communities. As discussed in the Introduction, Yellowstone prohibits the use of any fishing tackle containing lead. Fishing in Grand Teton National Park requires a Wyoming fishing license. Licenses may be purchased at the Moose Village Store, Signal Mountain Lodge, Colter Bay Marina, Flagg Ranch Village, and sporting goods stores.

Children under age 14 may also fish in North Elk Park Pond, located between the National Elk Refuge and U.S. 191 in Jackson, 11 miles south of Grand Teton National Park. This stocked pond was set aside as a training ground for young anglers.

For quick reference to trails offering fishing opportunities, check the Trip Finder in appendix A.

Climbing

Grand Teton National Park is a mecca for mountain climbers. The Tetons' soaring peaks pose challenges for climbers of every ability. All climbers are required to register prior to a climb. Register and obtain current route information at the Jenny Lake Ranger Station, (307) 733-2880. For families seeking climbing instruction or guided climbs, contact Exum Mountain Guides or Jackson Hole Mountain Guides. The Exum school offers daily basic and intermediate instruction within the park throughout the summer and private guides year round. For information contact Exum Mountain Guides, P.O. Box 56, Moose, WY 83012, (307) 733-2297; www.exumguides.com; or Jackson Hole Mountain Guides, P.O. Box 7477, Jackson, WY 83001, (307) 733-4979, www.jhmg.com.

For additional climbing experience and expert instruction, particularly in inclement weather, visit the Teton Rock Gym, an indoor climbing facility. Artificial-rock climbing walls pose challenges for novices and experts of all ages. The Teton Rock Gym is located in Jackson at 1116 Maple Way, (307) 733-0707.

Climbing is dangerous in Yellowstone due to loose and crumbly rock formations. Rock climbing is not recommended in most areas and is illegal in the Grand Canyon.

Biking

There are important restrictions on bicycling in Yellowstone and Grand Teton National Parks. In both parks, bicycling is strictly prohibited on hiking trails. Riding off-trail in the backcountry is also strictly prohibited. Before riding, check at a ranger station or visitor center for routes open to cyclists.

Riders must proceed with caution on park roads. Most have only narrow shoulders, and some have none at all. In July and August, RV traffic is heavy. Also, major road repairs occur every summer and fall, so check with a visitor center for road closures and delays before proceeding. In addition, drivers are easily distracted by scenery and wildlife, so cyclists must ride defensively.

Bike rentals for Grand Teton National Park are conveniently located at Dornan's in Moose (offering children's bikes and bike trailers), (307) 733-2522. Rentals are also available in Jackson Hole at Hoback Sports, 40 South Millward, (307) 733-2805); at Teton Cyclery, 175 North Glenwood Street (children's bikes and bike trailers), (307) 733-4386; and at Gart Sports, 455 West

Broadway, (307) 733-4449. During the summer, call ahead for reservations. Bike tours in both national parks are available from Teton Mountain Bike Tours, P.O. Box 7027, Jackson, WY 83001, (307) 733-0712, and from Fat Tire Tours, 40 South Millward Street, Jackson, WY 83001, (307) 733-5335.

Rodeos

The Jackson Hole Rodeo offers family entertainment every Wednesday and Saturday night throughout the summer. For ticket information, call (307) 733-2805. In addition, the world famous Cody Nite Rodeo performs nightly in Cody, WY, June through August. For information, call (307) 587-5155.

Rainy Day Recreation

In inclement weather, families can take cover in a variety of interesting places. Try the museums or park visitor centers listed in this chapter. To please active youngsters, visit the Teton Rock Gym or Jackson's fine new Recreation Center, which houses a gym and elaborate swimming facility, complete with hot tub and water slides. The Recreation Center is located at 155 East Gill Street in Jackson, just a few blocks north of the town square.

WILDLIFE VIEWING

One of the prime reasons to visit the GYE is to view its magnificent animals. From trumpeter swans to bull moose, the thrills are there for those who know when, where, and how to find them. To see as many animals as possible, put the following principles of wildlife observation to work. For maximum success, use them in conjunction with the Wildlife Locator and sample "safaris" found in appendix B.

Where to Look

To find a particular animal, know its habitat. The more you know about an animal's habitat, the easier it will be to locate the animal. Within their habitats, look for wildlife in "edge environments." Edge environments describe the areas where one habitat meets another, such as the transitional area between forest and meadow. Edge environments offer greater diversity of food and cover than either of the neighboring habitats. They therefore support greater numbers and kinds of animals. Areas that have a wealth of edge environments, like patchy forests broken by meadows or winding rivers with long shorelines, are productive areas for watching wildlife. Lush vegetation in these areas attracts large herbivores, such as deer and elk, and small mammals, such as rabbits and mice, who in turn attract predators such as hawks, weasels, and coyotes.

When to Look

Animals are diurnal (active during the day), nocturnal (active after dark), or crepuscular (active at sunrise and sunset). In general, the best time to view wildlife is shortly after dawn or at dusk when diurnal, nocturnal, and crepuscular animals mingle in a transitional time zone. In contrast, the least rewarding time is in the middle of the day. At high noon in the summer, when human activity is at its peak, animals generally avoid heat and activity and rest in day beds, out of sight.

In Yellowstone, spring and fall are the best times of year to see large numbers of elk, bison, moose, deer, bighorn sheep, and water birds. In summer, a large number of Yellowstone animals escape the heat and crowds by retreating to the backcountry. Nevertheless, observant and knowledgeable summer visitors can still see many animals by venturing into the park at dawn and dusk.

Moose, Grand Teton National Park

How to Look

Anyone serious about viewing wildlife should invest in a pair of good binoculars. Decent binoculars are available for less than $100, although the finest cost several times that much. Binoculars enable you to observe an animal without disturbing it. The most dedicated wildlife observers invest in a spotting scope. Although these are quite costly, their clarity and high level of magnification is invaluable for watching large predators such as bears and wolves.

When searching for animals, be alert to signs of their presence. If you can read animals' signs—tracks, scat, feeding debris, nests, and burrows—you can deduce their movements and activities without actually seeing them. With a little knowledge of droppings, for example, you can determine whether elk, moose, or deer favor the area. By noting the bark missing from a tree, you can tell whether bison or elk rubbed it or whether it was eaten by a porcupine. Sometimes seeing signs of an animal can be almost as exciting as seeing the animal itself. Fresh claw marks on a lodgepole, perhaps with some grizzly hair stuck to the oozing sap, is likely to impress most hikers.

Viewing Ethics

When you do find wildlife, observe unobtrusively *and from a distance*. An animal's survival may well depend on it. *If you cause an animal to move, you are too close.* Remember that animals usually feel anxious around humans. If an animal shows signs of agitation, leave immediately. Most animals live in a precarious balance between the demands of survival and the costs of obtaining enough food to survive. Even short interruptions of an animal's normal routine, when multiplied by a park full of curious visitors, can have deadly effects.

If you find young animals, leave them alone and do not linger. They were probably not abandoned. More likely, the mother is nearby. Your presence, however, may stop her from returning or may anger her enough to precipitate an attack. Fawns and elk calves are routinely left in the forest while their mothers feed. The odorless and camouflaged young usually go undetected by predators. If you happen to find one, or any other young animal, quickly leave the area.

CHAPTER

2

North Yellowstone

The northern portion of Yellowstone National Park is quietly scenic and wonderfully less congested than the central and southern portions of the park. With the exception of bustling Mammoth Hot Springs, the roads and trails are generally uncrowded. Its lower elevation makes it an excellent choice for spring and fall visits when snow covers trails in higher elevations.

Early summer is also a magical time here, for wildlife and wildflowers abound in the gorgeous, green Lamar Valley. Wildlife sightings in the valley include the newly introduced wolves, grizzlies, and black bears and the ever-present pronghorn, elk, mule deer, and bison. Even bighorn sheep may be glimpsed on cliffs near the North Entrance and occasionally at Calcite Springs Overlook on the Mammoth–Tower Road. Early morning and dusk are always the best times for viewing.

This area offers a variety of hiking trails, from easy outings (Trips 1, 2, 3, 6, 9, 10, 11) to more challenging climbs and descents (Trips 4, 5, 8). For a summer hike with a warm soak included, try strolling to "Boiling River" (Trip 2). For superb fishing, try Trips 5, 9, or 10. To visit the largest standing petrified forest in North America, try Trip 8. Those with strollers or wheelchairs can utilize the All Person's Nature Trail (Trip 6). Visitors seeking history as well as scenery should try Trip 7. Lastly, for great views of northern Yellowstone, climb Bunsen Peak (Trip 4). For information on current trail conditions, inquire at Albright Visitor Center in Mammoth or at Tower Ranger Station near Tower Junction.

If you have no time for hiking but want to make some roadside stops, try beautiful Undine Falls on the Mammoth–Tower Road; Tower Fall, just southeast of Tower Junction; and the Sheepeater Cliff Picnic Area on the Mammoth–Norris Road. The latter is one of the areas where the Sheepeater Indians resided before the creation of the park. Today it is a quietly beautiful area and good place to find yellow-bellied marmots.

Camping families have several options in North Yellowstone. For a measure of beauty and solitude, try Slough Creek Campground near the Lamar Valley. Its sites are attractively set along pretty Slough Creek. Another fine drive-in campground is Indian Creek Campground on the Mammoth–Norris Road.

1

Beaver Ponds Loop

DIFFICULTY: moderate
DISTANCE: 5 mile loop
USAGE: moderate
STARTING ELEVATION: 6,239 feet; elevation gain, 350 feet
SEASON: late May to early October
MAP: USGS 7.5-minute Mammoth, WY–MT

Escape busy Mammoth Hot Springs for a walk through grassy meadows and Douglas fir to a series of beaver ponds. You'll spy historic beaver dams and lodges, whose former inhabitants changed the landscape but have, most likely, moved on to new ponds. This trail is best hiked in spring or fall, when insects are minimal and wildlife abundant. In midsummer the trail is likely to be sunny and hot, so bring plenty of water.

Drive to Mammoth Hot Springs, 5 miles south of Yellowstone's North Entrance. To reach the trailhead, turn northwest on the road just south of the Mammoth Hot Springs Hotel (between the hotel and the dining room). Then take the first right and the next left. Look for the beginning of the unpaved Old Gardiner Road (on the slope immediately to the west). After you've located the road, you'll see the sign for the Beaver Ponds Trailhead, just above the road. Park in the large parking area directly adjacent. Walk up the Old Gardiner Road to begin the hike.

Almost immediately the trail leaves the road and heads left up the slope. Rise moderately among an abundance of waist-high sagebrush, rabbitbrush, and sun-loving flowers. To the east are steep cliffs known as the McMinn Bench, part of the northern flank of Mount Everts (7,841 feet). In spring, bighorn-sheep ewes and their lambs nimbly negotiate the precipitous slopes. With binoculars, you may spot them.

Follow the trail northwest traversing the hill. Then descend and cross a stream in the shade of Douglas fir. Soon pass under powerlines and climb again. In late summer enjoy fields of bright yellow Dalmatian toadflax, an exotic brought here from Eastern Europe. Exotics, or non-native plants, are often unwelcome and tenacious guests in the Greater Yellowstone Ecosystem. Seeds of exotics land in Yellowstone by a variety of means, including transport via bird and animal feces and adhesion to clothing and hay brought for horses. (For this reason, national parks require horses be fed only pellets within the park.) Hardy exotics crowd out rarer and less competitive native flowers and grasses and thus reduce the variety and amount of tasty forage for the park's wildlife.

Switchback up an open slope. To the left, note two small ponds that are prime watering holes for elk. At 2 miles from the trailhead, reach a bridge over the beaver pond's outlet creek. Shortly after, reach two ponds created by beaver dams. This is a good place to examine the work of these clever rodents or rest on the grassy shore and watch ducks cruise on the tranquil water.

The trail travels northwest around the pond past fields of flowers in late summer and early fall. Follow a creek bank covered with pink Canadian thistle and giant stalks of cow parsnip. Hardy cow parsnip can grow 6 feet tall. Its thick stalk is fuzzy, and its small white flowers are arranged in umbrella-shaped clusters. Today the park's wildlife enjoys this cousin of the carrot, but in earlier times, Native Americans also ate it (although it is reputed to be rather poor tasting). Find this remarkably large plant in wet areas throughout the park within the montane and subalpine zones.

At 2.5 miles, cross the stream and head south. In August, pass distinctive western coneflowers with their 2-inch-high brown cones on green stalks up to 5 feet tall. Below the coneflowers, large, red-orange Indian paintbrush thrive. *The Legend of the Indian Paintbrush*, a Native American tale retold and illustrated by Tomie DePaola, delightfully describes the "origin" of these colorful flowers (see appendix C).

Cross a series of bridges over wet meadows. Plant life is much different on the latter half of this hike due to the abundance of moisture. Watch for the round-leaf harebell whose five-petaled purple flowers hang gracefully down like delicate bells.

Next pass aspen whose trunks have been grazed by elk to a height of 7 to 8 feet. In winter when forage is scarce, elk eat the inner bark, leaving the tree scarred with large black patches. If elk strip too much bark off the slender aspen, the trees will die. Some naturalists see the abundance of blackened aspen as evidence that the park's large herds exceed the natural carrying capacity of the land. The reintroduction of wolves in 1995, the elk's

Pronghorn Antelope, Old Gardiner Road

natural predator, is expected to bring about a reduction of the Yellowstone elk population.

Ahead lies a beautiful golden field with widely spaced aspen and layers of blue mountains on the horizon beyond. Cross a dry, open slope with improving vistas. At about 4 miles from the start of the trail, the steam from Mammoth Hot Springs is visible. At 4.5 miles from the trailhead, its white terraces can be seen.

The Sepulcher Mountain Trail enters on the right and descends steeply, but continue left on the main trail. Shortly your trail also descends steeply in long switchbacks. Don't take short-cuts—this will only accelerate the erosion of the slope. After descending about 0.2 mile, reach a series of bridges and arrive at a rock chimney. Liberty Cap (the thumblike, protruding rock formation) is visible to the east. A right turn will take you to the Mammoth Hot Springs boardwalk and paved trail. To return to your car, walk east out to the road, turn left, and follow the road just 0.25 mile back to the trailhead at the Old Gardiner Road.

2

Boiling River

DIFFICULTY: very easy
DISTANCE: 0.5 mile one way
USAGE: high
STARTING ELEVATION: 5,500 feet; no elevation gain
SEASON: mid-May to early October
MAP: USGS 7.5-minute Mammoth,WY–MT

A short hike along the Gardner River takes visitors to "Boiling River," where a hot spring mixes with the cool river to create a natural hot tub. The lure of this warm dip is incredibly strong, for Yellowstone's waters tend toward the frigid. Boiling River thus draws crowds of one- to two- hundred people each summer day. For a bit of solitude, try this trail at dawn or in early autumn. In spring and early summer, the trail may be closed due to high water. It is critically important to follow all posted rules at Boiling River. The area has been significantly degraded due to high visitation; only your respect of its delicate beauty can hasten its restoration and preserve it for future generations. Also early in the season, be respectful and watchful of elk cows and calves who congregate along this section of the river.

The trailhead to Boiling River is located 2.6 miles south of Yellowstone's North Entrance and 2.2 miles north of Mammoth Hot Springs on the North Entrance Road (for trail map, see page 65). Look for signs indicating the 45th Parallel. Park in the lot on the east side of the road. Overflow parking is available on the road's west side.

Boiling River

The heavily traveled path to the "hot tub" parallels the Gardner River on its west bank. This river is a favorite for anglers. Its fast-flowing waters, gravelly bottom, and healthy vegetation supplies an excellent habitat for varieties of trout.

The area through which you are walking, the northwest corner of Yellowstone, is the lowest and the driest in the park, receiving less snow than surrounding areas. Consequently thousands of elk, bison, mule deer, pronghorn antelope, and bighorn sheep winter here. In summer, only the pronghorn remain in large numbers, most of the other animals climb to higher ground.

Follow the trail south along the riverbank. Across the river the rocky slopes of the McMinn Bench rise steeply. The cliffs are a spring calving area for bighorn sheep. These amazing climbers deftly negotiate the sheer slopes, successfully evading most four-legged predators. Despite their uncanny skill on the cliffs, the park's bighorn sheep are in trouble. In the late 1800s, hunters decimated the herds, and they never recovered. Bighorn sheep are extremely vulnerable to habitat disturbances and stress. Furthermore, they compete poorly with more robust elk for forage. In recent decades, disease has also diminished their numbers. Yellowstone's northwest herd hovers around 325. Your best chance of seeing this remarkable animal is on the summit of Mount Washburn (Trips 12 and 13). Remember, if you are lucky enough to see one, do not approach it! Despite your peaceful intentions, a close encounter will cause it severe stress.

After only a half mile of hiking, arrive at the famed Boiling River. Please respect the roped-off areas protecting the trampled vegetation. Watch children carefully. The currents of the Gardner

River are strong and could easily overpower a child. This is *not* a safe swimming area. Furthermore, the NPS recommends that you keep your head above water at all times and do not allow the thermally heated water to enter your mouth or nose. The warm waters may contain bacteria that cause severe skin rashes or infectious and/or amoebic meningitis.

Without the crowds, the Boiling River is quite lovely and immensely enjoyable. From May through September, there are a variety of wildflowers. In any season, the glimpse of a bald eagle, hunting coyote, or graceful elk from the hot tub completes a perfect picture.

3

Mammoth Hot Springs Lower Terraces

DIFFICULTY: very easy
DISTANCE: 0.75 mile one way
USAGE: high
STARTING ELEVATION: 6,239 feet; elevation gain,
    175 feet
SEASON: mid-May through October
MAP: USGS 7.5-minute Mammoth, WY–MT

Strolling the boardwalk of Mammoth Hot Springs Lower Terrace is a must for all visitors to the area. Join a ranger-led hike or take a self-guided tour with the aid of the Yellowstone Association's informative brochure (available at trailside dispensers). In spring and fall, hikers share the boardwalk with elk and often bison. This makes the walk especially delightful, but remember, do not approach closer than 25 yards under any circumstances. Also, never allow children to leave the boardwalk and risk injury on unstable ground.

Drive to Mammoth Hot Springs, 5 miles south of the North Entrance. The boardwalks of the Mammoth Hot Springs Lower Terraces are located just south of the Mammoth Hot Springs Hotel. At the beginning of the boardwalk, pick up the brochure describing the features of the terraces and the process by which they were created. In short, hot gases beneath the earth heat water (from rain and melted snow) that seeps through fissures in the ground. The heated water dissolves buried deposits of limestone, and then carries the dissolved minerals to the surface. When the hot water reaches the surface, some of the minerals it carries are precipitated out and deposited as ivory travertine. After years and years of deposition, a travertine limestone "wedding cake" forms. In geologic time, this build-up is exceedingly rapid, averaging 8 inches of deposited rock per year. Some years, up to 22 inches of rock is deposited at Mammoth, up to 2 tons of travertine per day!

Despite all the obvious thermal activity, visitors will find no geysers in the Mammoth area. This is because the water is not hot

Taking the temperature of thermal pool on ranger-led hike—never approach a pool without a ranger!

enough. The origin of Mammoth's hot springs is the Norris Geyser Basin, 21 miles away. Mammoth's distance from the source of heat at Norris is just enough to reduce the water temperature below the boiling point. In fact, none of the bubbling hot springs at Mammoth contain boiling water. The bubbling action that looks like boiling is caused by carbon dioxide gas expanding at the surface (like the bubbles in a glass of soda pop). This water, nevertheless, is still incredibly dangerous. It is easily hot enough to cause severe burns upon contact!

As hot springs flow over the white terraces, colorful bacteria and algae grow in the water, creating a fantastic spectrum of color. The temperature of the hot springs determines the particular type of bacteria that can survive in the water. Bacteria differ in color, so you can guess the temperature of the water with a fair degree of accuracy by looking at the color of its bacteria or algae. For example, yellow indicates water of about 167 degrees F, blue indicates a temperature of about 160 degrees F, and orange-brown indicates a temperature of 130 degrees F.

Around the hot springs, notice the many standing dead trees with white bases. These are "bobby sock trees," actually tree skeletons "cemented" in place by the travertine. Bobby sock trees were killed by the mineral-laden hot water. When the tree's roots drew up the water, the minerals solidified within the tree, eventually killing it by turning its inner workings to stone from the base up. Bobby sock trees are a sure sign of past or present thermal activity.

One of the most amazing things about Mammoth Hot Springs is its never-ending evolution. Boardwalks frequently need to be removed or re-routed because of changes in thermal activity. A colorful pool this year may change the next year beyond recognition. Changes are caused by shifts in the underground plumbing, changes in water temperature, or blockage of water sources. Mild earthquakes common to the area can initiate the changes. Think of Mammoth Hot Springs as an artist's work in progress, and enjoy this living sculpture garden.

To see more fascinating hot springs and travertine formations, visit the Mammoth Hot Springs Upper Terraces that begin at the top of the Lower Terraces boardwalk. This is most easily done by vehicle via Upper Terrace Drive. The one-way road (1.5 miles) starts about 1 mile south of the Lower Terrace Parking Area on the road to Norris. For a more intimate view of Mammoth's Upper Terrace, take a guided walk with a ranger to view backcountry thermal features seldom seen by the general public. Inquire at the Albright Visitor Center for a schedule of tours.

4

Bunsen Peak

DIFFICULTY: strenuous
DISTANCE: 2.2 miles one way
USAGE: moderate
STARTING ELEVATION: 7,320 feet; elevation gain, 1,345 feet
SEASON: mid-June through September
MAP: USGS 7.5-minute Mammoth, WY–MT

For the most commanding view in this region, climb Bunsen Peak. Its summit affords glorious views of the Yellowstone Valley, Mammoth Hot Springs, the mysterious Hoodoos, Swan Lake Flat, the Gallatins, and Mount Washburn. After the 1988 fires burned its slopes, these views were significantly improved. This hike is a tough family climb, but worth the effort, especially in the early morning. If you're hiking early in the season, use care crossing snow patches.

From Mammoth Hot Springs, drive about 5 miles south on the Mammoth–Norris Road. Just after passing the Golden Gate and Rustic Falls, look for a turnout on the left (east) side of the highway. Park, walk past the barricade, and hike on the closed road briefly until you see the Bunsen Peak Trail entering on the left.

The trail winds through burned lodgepole pine forest, soon climbing by switchbacks up the west slope of Bunsen Peak. You gain altitude swiftly, and with each footstep the views improve. Look west over Gardner's Hole, where fur trapper Johnson Gardner trapped extensively in the 1830s. In the Hole lies Swan Lake, where trumpeter swans occasionally nest in the summer.

In the burned forest black sculptural forms stand. Beneath bare branches, newly enriched soil and the infusion of sunlight nourishes a variety of flowers. Look for red-orange Indian paintbrush and lavender lupine. Lupine was originally believed to be a noxious weed that stole valuable nutrients from the soil. For that

View west from Bunsen Peak

reason, Europeans named the flower after the Latin word for wolf, *lupus*, for they considered the wolf also evil and destructive. We now know that both theories were far from the truth; lupine actually enriches poor soils, and wolves, of course, play an invaluable role in the ecosystem.

Soon a switchback brings you north to a dramatic overlook of Cathedral Rock, an impressive rock spire, and the Hoodoos, a jumble of travertine boulders. The Hoodoos are actually the ruins of an ancient terrace altered by hot springs. Below and beyond the Hoodoos lie Mammoth Hot Springs. Continue to rise and cross several talus slopes. Pass impressive Douglas fir as great views open again to the southwest. Far to the west rise the peaks of the Gallatin Range.

Near the top the switchbacks steepen. Stay on the trail, for talus slopes and snow patches can be treacherous. (Near the top, find

NPS radio relaying equipment. Please stay clear.) At the summit, look east for views of the Washburn Range, northwest for an impressive view of Electric Peak (named for its propensity to be struck by lightning) and south to the Tetons, which can be seen on a clear day.

Geologists believe Bunsen Peak is the cone of an ancient volcano. The peak was named for Robert Bunsen, the first scientist to conduct an in-depth study of the workings of geysers, and who also invented the Bunsen burner, a common piece of laboratory equipment. Lastly, look south to find the steam rising from Norris Geyser Basin. This is exactly how it was found by white men. In 1872, two expedition members climbed Bunsen Peak and "discovered" the immense and active basin.

Return carefully to the trailhead by retracing your steps. When you reach the bottom, look for bison that often travel the unpaved road.

Blacktail Deer Creek

DIFFICULTY: strenuous
DISTANCE: 3.7 miles one way
USAGE: moderate
STARTING ELEVATION: 6,900 feet; elevation loss, 1,100 feet
SEASON: mid-May through early October
MAP: USGS 7.5-minute Blacktail Deer Creek, WY

Brave a long descent along Blacktail Deer Creek to visit Yellowstone's magnificent Black Canyon. Along the way pass through gentle meadows, visit a small cascade, and try some fine fishing. Flower displays are excellent in July. Backpacking families can find a creekside campsite less than 2 fairly level miles from the trailhead. Hikers must be sure to bring plenty of water and save some energy for the arduous climb out.

Drive 6.5 miles west from Tower Junction on the Mammoth–Tower Road to a small parking area on the north side of the road (between Blacktail Pond and Blacktail Deer Creek) signed for the Blacktail Creek Trail. From Mammoth, drive 11.5 miles on the Mommoth–Tower Road east to find the trailhead.

The trail heads directly north past shallow ponds and climbs a gentle rise. Pass between two "exclosures," areas fenced by the NPS to study the impacts of grazing and browsing mammals such as elk, bison, deer, and moose. Where these animals are plentiful, young aspen are greedily munched before they have a chance to mature.

Just after the exclosures, descend to a trail junction with the Rescue Creek Trail on the left, 0.7 mile from the trailhead. Continue straight. A multitude of flowers adorn the rolling meadows. Look for lavender lupine, creamy buckwheat, and low-lying pink bitterroot, Montana's state flower. The roots of the bitterroot were an important source of food for Native Americans. The origin of this flower is explained by a Flathead Indian legend. It tells of an old woman whose family was starving to death. Seeing her crying, a spirit bird came to her rescue, and everywhere her tears fell, a nutritious bitterroot bloomed.

Examining aspen bark eaten by elk

Also along the trail are plentiful Unita ground squirrels, who stand on their hind legs before diving into their burrows. Numerous, too, are the large elliptical holes dug by badgers. Badgers are far more secretive than the ubiquitous squirrels, so consider yourself lucky if the large, masked rodent shows its belligerent head.

The trail heads toward rushing Blacktail Deer Creek. The creek was named for the deer who frequent this section of the park. The park's deer, however, are actually Rocky Mountain mule deer and not true blacktail deer, which are found primarily on the West Coast. Look for the deer at dawn and dusk in edge environments, where the forest meets meadows or streams.

At approximately 1.75 miles from the trailhead, a spur trail leads down to a campsite by Blacktail Deer Creek. The main trail continues to descend, paralleling the creek. Anglers may be trying for brook and cutthroat trout along the banks, although the more coveted spots are closer to the creek's junction with the Yellowstone River. Just after the campsite watch for a second spur trail to Black-tail Falls, a nice cascade that provides a good spot to rest.

Evidence of the 1988 fire is apparent on the slopes above the creek. Walk through skeleton forests of Douglas fir whose barkless snags raise bare, whitened branches. Across the creek, notice the pillarlike rock formation high above the water. This is an example of columnar basalt, a formation resulting from cooling lava flows.

The descent becomes steeper as you approach the Yellowstone River and Black Canyon. The trail loses nearly 900 feet in the last 1.5 miles. Those who take the plunge are well-rewarded. The trail affords beautiful views of the powerful Yellowstone River and Black Canyon's magnificent rock walls. Bighorn sheep are occasionally spotted on the cliffs. A suspension bridge provides access across the river. For those with additional energy, Crevice Lake lies just 0.25 mile to the west on the Yellowstone River Trail and Knowles Falls is found just 1.25 miles beyond that. All others should retrace their steps to the trailhead, allowing plenty of time and water for the climb back.

6

All Person's Nature Trail

DIFFICULTY: very easy; handicapped accessible with
   assistance
DISTANCE: 0.5 mile loop
USAGE: low
STARTING ELEVATION: 800 feet; no elevation gain
SEASON: mid-May through early October
MAP: USGS 7.5-minute Tower Junction, WY

This boardwalk enables visitors to tour a forest burned in Yellowstone's 1988 fires. Interpretive signs encourage visitors to explore the many forces of nature, including fire, which shape a landscape. While most children are familiar with Smokey Bear and the story of Bambi, few know the positive side of forest fires. Walking this boardwalk is a good introduction.

All Person's Nature Trail

Drive 8.1 miles east of Mammoth Hot Springs or 9.9 miles west of Tower Junction on the Mammoth–Tower Road. Park in the turnout on the north side of the road. Begin on the boardwalk and walk clockwise.

Of the eight major fires that swept through Yellowstone in 1988, the one that burned the most acreage, including this area, was the North Fork Fire. From its discovery on July 22, 1988, until its smoldering demise 2 months later, the North Fork Fire consumed nearly 500,000 acres, more than half of the total acreage burned in Yellowstone that summer.

The North Fork Fire was started by a logger who discarded a lit cigarette just outside the park's southwest boundary. The National Park Service fought the fire immediately, but all attempts to subdue it were futile. Extreme drought conditions had so dried the forests that the trees lit up like match sticks. High winds drove embers over natural and man-made firebreaks. Backfires and firelines were useless. In short, the North Fork Fire was uncontrollable.

Before the fires of 1988, much of Yellowstone was covered with dense stands of lodgepole pine. Unfortunately, many of these forests were not healthy. Years of fire suppression by the park service had created unnaturally old and uniformly aged stands. In the first hundred years of Yellowstone Park, the park's policy was to extinguish quickly all fires. The resulting densely packed trees were highly susceptible to disease and insect infestation. In the decades before the fire, pine beetles took great advantage of the weakened trees and killed a large percentage. Forests filled with standing dead and dying trees were ripe for burning when the North Fork Fire arrived.

Furthermore, historians claim that significant fires occur every 250 to 400 years in the Greater Yellowstone Ecosystem. Growth rings on the park's oldest trees reveal that a great fire had not swept the park since the early 1700s. Historically, Yellowstone was due for a fire.

The North Fork Fire was not an ecological catastrophe. As early as the spring of 1989, lush regrowth was already apparent. Along the boardwalk, notice the abundant pink fireweed and lavender lupine. Here and throughout the park, fireweed moved in rapidly to protect the soil from erosion. The vibrant pink flower takes its name from its rapid invasion of fire-ravaged or disturbed areas. Lupine also came to the rescue by trapping nitrogen and returning it to the soil, thus aiding the growth of new plants. Look also for heart-leafed arnica, with its yellow daisylike flower. Arnica is another early pioneer that holds and enriches the soil.

A profusion of young lodgepole pine also grow along the boardwalk. These pines are specially adapted to fire. They bear serotinous cones that open and release their seeds only under conditions of extreme heat. The post-fire conditions of bare mineral soil and full sunlight is their prescription for rapid growth. The pines will rise quickly over the next 30 to 80 years. Children walking the boardwalk today who return with their own children will walk, 25 years hence, beneath these trees rather than above them.

Wildlife, also, is faring well in post-fire Yellowstone. The dead trees that surround the boardwalk are a haven for insects. The insects attract birds such as woodpeckers and bluebirds, who make their homes in the standing snags. The young nutritious plants blanketing the ground attract marmots, mule deer, elk, and a host of small rodents. The rodents in turn are food for coyotes, hawks, and owls. Contrary to the message found in popular children's tales, most wildlife prospers from periodic forest fires. Their mobility saves them from harm during the actual burn.

Compared to the dense, dark forest that stood here before 1988, this area is filled with diversity, life, and potential. The burned area supplies food and homes to many more animals and opens up vistas that were blocked for hundreds of years. While it is natural to mourn destruction, it is wise to champion rebirth and understand the natural healing process already well under way in Yellowstone.

———————————— 7 ————————————

Yellowstone River Overlook

DIFFICULTY: easy
DISTANCE: 2 miles one way
USAGE: low
STARTING ELEVATION: 6,270 feet; elevation gain, 200 feet
SEASON: mid-May to early October
MAPS: USGS 7.5-minute Tower Junction and Specimen Creek, WY

This short trail brings you to an impressive overlook of the Yellowstone River at the Grand Canyon's northern end. Walking along the canyon rim, 700 feet above the river, there is opportunity to see bighorn sheep on the cliffs, mule deer or elk in the meadows, and countless marmots on trailside rocks.

Drive 1.5 miles east from Tower Junction on Tower-Northeast Entrance Road to the Yellowstone River Picnic Area on the right (south) side of the road. Park in the picnic area and look for the signed trail that heads southeast, ascending the hill behind the picnic area. (The trailhead sign indicates the junction with Specimen Ridge Trail in 2 miles.)

The trail climbs the grassy slope, thick with sagebrush and flowers in summer. Douglas fir dot the hillside, easily recognized by their soft needles and distinctive cones with tiny trident-shaped bracts protruding from their scales. One Yellowstone ranger imaginatively likened the tridents to the backsides (two back legs and a tail) of tiny mice jumping into holes between the scales—an excellent description for children.

The trail quickly reaches the rim of the canyon. Below, to your right the Yellowstone River flows rapidly north. Walk east along the rim to enjoy the magnificent views. All around notice the glacial erratics (large boulders) dotting the hillsides and meadows.

The erratics were dropped by the huge glaciers that shaped the valley. Note also that many erratics have a tree growing from their north sides. Boulders shelter seedlings from damaging winds, allowing them to flourish.

In early summer, arrowleaf balsamroot adorns the hillside. The large, yellow heads bloom in luxurious bunches. The flowers are easily identified by their arrowhead-shaped leaves. Young shoots are a favorite early summer treat of elk and deer. Native Americans also had many uses for this plant: a healing poultice was made from its leaves, its seeds and woody roots were roasted, and its ripe stem was peeled and eaten raw like celery. By July their bright heads shrivel to brown as these dry slopes welcome smaller and more subtle flowers.

Soon arrive at an area with an abundance of rocks and a large number of yellow-bellied marmots. Each morning, chunky marmots waddle from their rocky burrows to eat the nearby vegetation. By September their summer munching has added half an inch of fat all over their round bodies. Roly-poly marmots are a favorite prey of golden eagles.

The trail continues southeast along the canyon rim. Across the river the geothermal activity of Calcite Springs comes into view. This is an excellent place to see how heat and water dramatically change the appearance of rock. On cliffs opposite the springs, bighorn sheep can be seen in early summer and fall. As you walk, notice also the dark holes at the top of the cliffs, marked by white bird droppings. These are nests of ravens, the huge black birds seen throughout the park.

"The Narrows" of the Yellowstone River

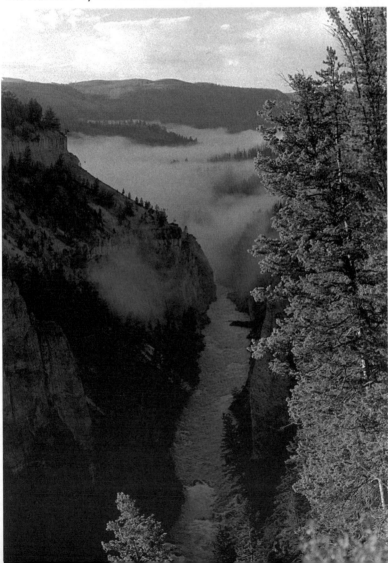

The trail approaches "The Narrows," the narrowest section of the 14-mile-long Grand Canyon. Proceed to the junction with the Specimen Ridge Trail, 2 miles from the trailhead. Riverside at this point, you are directly opposite the Tower Fall parking lot. History enters here, just east (upstream) of Tower Creek's entrance into the Yellowstone River. There you'll find the site of the "Bannock Ford."

From 1840 to 1878, at this relatively narrow and shallow section, Indians, including the Bannock, crossed the river to enter their summer hunting grounds. The scarcity of bison in the west drove the Bannock and neighboring tribes to seek bison herds in the east. The ford was part of the 200-mile trail across northern Yellowstone used by the Indians. The trail was only in use for about 40 years, for by 1878, the government had forced the Bannock and other tribes onto reservations. Nevertheless, the trail is permanently a part of Yellowstone, for the present-day road from Mammoth to Cooke City closely follows the original Bannock Trail. The trail junction is a good place to turn around. Retrace your steps and enjoy the views as you head back to the trailhead.

8

Petrified Forest

DIFFICULTY: strenuous
DISTANCE: 1.75 miles one way
USAGE: Low
STARTING ELEVATION: 6,200 feet; elevation gain, 1,150 feet
SEASON: late-May to mid-September
MAP: USGS 7.5-minute Tower Junction, WY

High on an exposed ridge, reachable only by rugged, off-trail hiking, are some of the finest specimens of petrified trees on earth. Fifty-five million years ago, a tremendous rain of volcanic ash buried alive an immense standing deciduous forest. Beneath the ash, the trees absorbed silica and thus solidified in their original form. Some specimens stand 15 feet high on the eroded slopes.

Finding the trees in their remote and somewhat hidden location heightens the hiker's sense of mystery and discovery. In addition, numerous fascinating fossil imprints can be found on the surrounding volcanic rocks.

Finding the trees, however, requires a steep climb and some cross-country hiking. A steep, badly eroded trail leads straight up the ridge but this is *not* the recommended route. Continued use will only make this trail more treacherous. Those interested in visiting the forest should stop at the nearby Ranger Station at Tower Junction, where the ranger will explain the best route to the forest and supply you with a map.

This area is well-frequented by bears, so take appropriate precautions. Lastly, remember, of course, that it is illegal to remove specimens from the park. Carrying away even a small fragment degrades the area and adversely affects scientific research there.

9

Slough Creek Meadows

DIFFICULTY: easy
DISTANCE: 2 miles one way
USAGE: moderate
STARTING ELEVATION: 6,400 feet; elevation gain, 300 feet
SEASON: mid-May through late September
MAP: USGS 7.5-minute Tower Junction, WY

The Slough Creek Meadows Trail provides access to a gentle and beautiful valley, much favored by fishermen. This easy hike offers flowers in summer, bright aspen in fall, and curvaceous, trout-filled Slough Creek and snow-capped Cutoff Mountain year round. Bring bug repellent in summer.

Drive east on the Tower–Northeast Entrance Road approximately 5.7 miles from Tower Junction to the dirt road leading to Slough Creek Campround. Turn north on this road and drive about 1.8 miles to the signed trailhead, located about 0.5 mile before the campground.

Ascend on the Douglas fir-lined road, passing groves of blackened aspen whose inner bark has been eaten by elk. Creamy buckwheat, pink sticky geranium, lavender lupine, and bright yellow arrowleaf balsamroot decorate the meadows. Colorful butterflies also abound in summer. Yellowstone hosts at least 128 species of butterflies; this is a good hike for children to start counting.

Have children also look on the hillsides for "lollipop" trees, where elk have browsed so heavily on a tree's lower branches that the tree is shaped like a lollipop, with a bare trunk extending down from a roundish clump of vegetation. In winter, when food is scarce, elk will chew on nearly any plant.

After nearly a mile, the trail levels, descends a bit, and bends north. Pass a very wet area to your right, perfect moose habitat, where there's likely to be at least one family of ducks. To the north, your first good view of Cutoff Mountain appears.

The trail next descends gently into a shady forest of fir and spruce, and then quickly reaches the "First Meadow" of Slough Creek. Explore the meadow by bearing right at the trail junction. The Buffalo Ford Trail heads left.

Slough Creek meadow is lovely and peaceful, framed by exquisite silhouettes of mountains to the north. On its green banks, anglers try for rainbow and cutthroat trout. You may also meet the stagecoach that works the wagon trail, bringing guests to the Silver Tip Ranch located just outside the park boundary.

Further exploration brings you to the Slough Creek Patrol Cabin. This is a good turnaround point for the youngest hikers. Those hungry for more meadows (or fishing) can follow the trail north over a 200-foot rise to the "Second Meadow," another fine spot to fish or picnic.

10

Trout Lake

DIFFICULTY: easy
DISTANCE: 0.5 mile one way
USAGE: high
STARTING ELEVATION: 6,800 feet; elevation gain, 150 feet
SEASON: early June to mid-September
MAP: USGS 7.5-minute Mount Hornaday, WY

Trout Lake delivers a nice scenic punch. The perfectly round lake is gorgeously set beneath snow-capped peaks, amid gently sloping flowered meadows. Arrive when the trout are spawning and you can watch them lying in the outlet stream, flipping like pancakes. For those who have never seen multitudes of beautiful

To Northeast Entrance

Tower-Northeast Entrance Road

Trout Lake

N

0   .5

MILES

To Tower

fish up close and wild, Trout Lake is a real treat. Be forewarned that Trout Lake is a popular fishing destination. You'll share the lake with numerous biting insects also, so be prepared.

Drive approximately 17.7 miles from Tower Junction on the Tower–Northeast Entrance Road to a pullout with a trailhead sign on the left side of the road. From the Northeast Entrance, the trailhead is about 1.5 miles south of the Pebble Creek Campground. Park in the small pullout and find the trail on the pullout's west side.

The trail climbs moderately amid flowers and mature Douglas fir. Watch for pink sticky geranium, vivid blue forget-me-nots, and pastel pink phlox. Butterflies are especially attracted to the phlox's narrow tube where its nectar is stored. Sample the fragrance of this small, five-petaled flower. It is said to be particularly sweet at dusk.

A short climb quickly brings you over a small ridge to the lake. Trout Lake is scenically nestled amid the surrounding peaks of Druid Peak, Frederick Peak, and Mount Hornaday. Mount Hornaday was named for a naturalist instrumental in the fight to save the bison from extinction. A fine trail runs the perimeter of the lake, allowing for easy exploring.

The finest area for picnics is on the far side of the lake, where you have an impressive view of the Thunderer (10,243 feet). This formidable peak was named for its attraction of sensational lightning strikes. To reach the lake's opposite shore, turn right, avoiding the spillway that was built when this lake supported a hatchery. Along the way, pass the inlet creek, where just a bit upstream, spawning rainbow trout can be seen in mid-June. Please don't unduly disturb the fish. This lake was once over-fished and is now strictly catch-and-release. Its rainbows are quite hefty.

Families should venture all the way around the lake. Ducks, trout, and anglers may be all the wildlife visible at midday, but deer, elk, and bear may be present in the quiet hours. Hikers may also explore this beautiful area further by hiking off-trail in the surrounding meadows.

Tower Fall

DIFFICULTY: very easy
DISTANCE: 0.5 mile one way
USAGE: high
STARTING ELEVATION: 6,800 feet; elevation loss, 200 feet
SEASON: late May-early October
MAP: USGS 7.5-minute Tower Junction, WY

A well-maintained trail leads to the base of Tower Fall, where torrents of water leap through tall, rock pinnacles. The best time to hike this trail is in spring and early summer, when the water is high, and in the early morning, when the sun casts a gorgeous rainbow. In summer, the *only* time to visit the falls is at dawn or dusk, for crowds easily overwhelm this short trail.

Drive to the Tower Fall Parking Area, located 2.5 miles southeast of Tower Junction on the Tower–Canyon Road. The trail starts on the paved path to the right of the Hamilton Store (for trail map, see page 81).

Walk down the path to the fall overlook, and then head to the right and descend on a staired trail. The trail is easy, but steep in places as it winds down through juniper and Douglas fir. Arrive first at a bench overlooking the Yellowstone River. Across the river, the yellow rock cliffs of Specimen Ridge rise almost 700 feet above the water. Ocher sandstone cliffs like these along the lower reaches of the Yellowstone River inspired the Minnetaree Indians to call the river *Mi tsi a-da-zi* or Rock Yellow River. The French recorded the name as R. Des Roches Jaunes (River of Yellow Rock). In 1798 the name was translated into English as Yellow Stone.

A short distance upstream lies the Bannock Ford, where between 1840 and 1878, Native American tribes crossed the Yellowstone River to visit their summer hunting grounds (see Trip 7). It is also likely that John Colter, the first white man to enter Yellowstone, crossed the Yellowstone River at the Bannock Ford when he arrived in 1807.

To view Tower Fall, continue along the main trail (to the left). A few minutes' hiking upstream along Tower Creek brings you to the base of the fall. One hundred and thirty-two feet above you, water rushes between dark stone pillars. The eroding force of water and the differing resistance of the underlying rock created the falls and columns. The strangely eroded "towers" above the fall give the place a mystical feel. Around you, lush, green vegetation and colorful flowers are nurtured by the waterfall's spray. When sufficiently cooled by the spray, retrace your steps to return to the parking area.

Tower Fall

CHAPTER

3

Central Yellowstone

The foremost attractions of Central Yellowstone are the magnificent Grand Canyon of the Yellowstone River, fascinating Norris Geyser Basin, and wildlife-filled Hayden Valley. This chapter describes many beautiful hikes in this region and one very challenging mountain bike route.

North of the Grand Canyon, on the Tower–Canyon Road, lie the trailheads for Mount Washburn, a popular and terrifically scenic destination. Summit climbers are rewarded with unparalled views of the park and surrounding mountain ranges. Try it by bike (Trip 13) or by foot (Trip 12). The meadows on the north side of Mount Washburn are excellent places to look for grizzly bears from the turnouts on Tower–Canyon Road.

The Grand Canyon offers many trails around its rim, from the relatively easy (Trips 15, 16) to the moderately strenuous (Trip 17, 18) to the most challenging (Trip 14). If there is no time for hiking in this region, the most impressive canyon viewpoints are the north rim's Brink of Lower Falls Trail (Trip 16), which takes you to the dizzying edge of the magnificent Lower Falls, and the south rim's Artist Point overlook, where a panoramic view of the canyon and Lower Falls can be seen. Artist Point is especially breathtaking in early morning and at sunset.

Just south of Canyon Village, on the Canyon–Fishing Bridge

Road, lies bison-filled Hayden Valley. This 9-mile-long valley hosts over 1,000 bison, and numerous elk, grizzlies, and bald eagles from spring through the fall. During the bison's rut in August, driving is difficult, for the feisty bison often stubbornly occupy the roadway, generating "buffalo jams."

Just south of the Hayden Valley, Le Hardy Rapids deserves a short visit if you're touring the park during trout spawning season in early summer. At the height of the season, trout can be seen jumping the rapids 3 to 4 feet in the air, about every 15 seconds. A boardwalk takes visitors to a beautiful viewpoint right above the rapids.

Norris Geyser Basin offers great opportunities to view geysers and colorful hot-springs-viewing on an expansive system of boardwalks. Don't miss the eruption of Echinus Geyser, whose 20-minute show rightfully draws substantial crowds. Check for predicted eruption times at the Norris Museum. To see fascinating geothermal features without the crowds, hike the Artist Paint Pots Trail (Trip 19). Camping families can find scenic riverside campsites at nearby Norris Campground.

Finally, those with strollers or wheelchairs can take the handicapped-accessible Two Ribbons Trail (Trip 20) and examine the jubilant rebirth of a burned forest along the beautiful Madison River.

Norris Geyser Basin, Yellowstone National Park

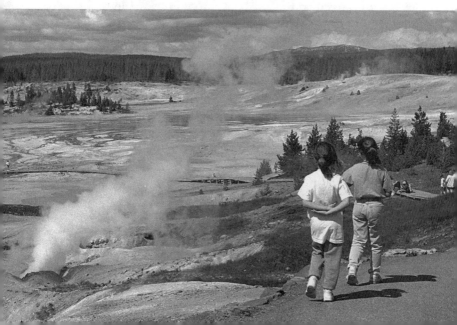

12

Mount Washburn

DIFFICULTY: strenuous
DISTANCE: 3 miles one way
USAGE: high
STARTING ELEVATION: 8,863 feet; elevation gain,
    1,380 feet
SEASON: late June to September
MAP: USGS 7.5-minute Mount Washburn, WY

This is a great climb for families. Strong youngsters can handle the grade, the views are fabulous, and an enclosed fire lookout on the summit shields you from the roaring winds. Hikers also have a good chance of seeing Yellowstone's elusive bighorn sheep—reason enough to climb 1,400 feet to the summit.

Drive to Dunraven Pass Picnic Area, located 5.6 miles north of Canyon Village and 13.4 miles south of Tower Junction on the Canyon–Tower Road. Park in the lot on the east side of the road. In early summer, check for snow conditions prior to hiking. Even in midsummer, enough snow may linger for a few snowballs at the top.

This route to the summit follows an old road with a moderate grade. With each step, views improve and trailside flowers grow more abundant. Flower displays are quite grand in midsummer. Growing in profusion are red-orange Indian paintbrush, lavender lupine, and yellow windflowers. In early summer, pink shooting stars brighten the meadows.

Notice the abundance of whitebark pine lining the trail. Many were touched by the sweeping North Fork Fire in the summer of 1988 (see Trip 6). Recognize whitebark pine by its needles in bundles of five and its short, purplish cones. Whitebark pine seeds are an important food source for the park's grizzlies.

Two other woodland creatures, the red squirrel and Clark's nutcracker, also depend on the nutritious, high-fat seeds. Instead of competing, however, both of these creatures inadvertently assist the grizzly. First, in a good year, a red squirrel gathers and hides thousands of cones in middens (huge storage piles) in the whitebark forest. Bears have only to find these treasure troves to

To Tower Junction

Chittenden Road Lower Parking Area (if road is closed)

Chittenden Road

Chittenden Road Upper Parking Area

Canyon-Tower Road

Trip 12

N

0 1

MILES

Mount Washburn bike route

Fire Lookout

Mount Washburn 10,243

No bikes allowed

Dunraven Pass Picnic Area

Trip 12

To Canyon Village

satisfy their voracious appetites. An indiscriminate (and ungrateful) bear will also dine on the red squirrel!

The Clark's nutcracker enters the picture by extracting thousands of pine seeds with its long, pointed beak. The bird then stores these seeds in underground caches. When the cone crop is good, a single Clark's nutcracker can remove over thirty thousand seeds! More importantly, the birds misplace half of the seeds they bury. Thus, many germinate, ensuring a continuing source of food. Many other forest animals enjoy the whitebark seeds, but none are so essential to the grizzly's survival as the industrious nutcracker and red squirrel.

The trail climbs steadily in long switchbacks up the ancient volcano. To the east, there are increasingly good views of the jagged Absaroka Range, named for the Crow Indians in their native language. On a clear day, look south for a distant view of the Grand Tetons. As you near the summit, scan the slopes for bighorn sheep. The sheep are frequently seen, often quite near the trail. If you encounter a herd, use binoculars, and do not approach them. The animals are quite vulnerable to stress.

Regal bighorn rams can be recognized by their C-shaped headdress of horns. Bighorn sheep, both male and female, grow horns from birth, but only the males' horns reach majestic proportions. The oldest rams have nearly a full circle of horn, while young rams have short, straight horns. Young males, in fact, are easily mistaken for ewes (occasionally even by the other rams!).

In summer, the approach to the summit is bordered by ground-hugging, alpine flowers. Don't tread on these fragile beauties. In their extremely short growing season of just a few weeks, the flowers must grow, bloom, and set seed. Some of these tiny plants are actually decades old!

Finally, atop the summit, take in the fabulous view, and then duck out of the wind by visiting the fire lookout, open June through September. In the lookout's observation room are natural history displays and a powerful telescope. Be sure to bring a good map so you can locate landmarks from this central vantage point. To the east is the Grand Canyon of the Yellowstone, to the south Hayden Valley and Yellowstone Lake, and to the southwest Old Faithful and the Lower, Middle, and Upper Geyser basins.

The summit of Mount Washburn is a great place to contemplate the Yellowstone caldera, for Mount Washburn sits on its northeast rim. Six hundred thousand years ago, an immense dome rose up and exploded in one of the greatest volcanic eruptions ever to occur on earth. Debris landed as far away as present-day Kansas. It is said that the volume of lava and ash hurled was ten thousand times greater than the 1980 eruption of Mount St. Helens. After the eruption, the dome collapsed, leaving a crater, or caldera, measuring nearly 50 miles across. This caldera was once thousands of feet deep, but subsequent lava flows and glacial sculpting have filled in most of the depression. Look south from the summit to the vast forested interior of Yellowstone and you'll be looking at the area encompassed by the immense crater. Retrace your steps to return to the trailhead and enjoy gorgeous views all the way down.

13

Mount Washburn

DIFFICULTY: strenuous
DISTANCE: 3 miles one way
USAGE: high
STARTING ELEVATION: 8,840 feet; elevation gain, 1,440 feet
SEASON: late June to September
MAP: USGS 7.5-minute Mount Washburn, WY

Strong mountain bikers can pedal to the finest lookout in Yellowstone via Mount Washburn's Chittenden Road. From the spectacular summit, take in the Absarokas, the Gallatins and even the Tetons, and then prime yourself for a thrilling ride down, dropping 1,400 feet in 3 miles. Good brakes and self-control are essential on this busy trail. In early summer, cyclists should check road conditions before departing. This route is also recommended for hikers in early summer when the trail from Dunraven Pass (Trip 12) is impassable due to snowfields. Finally, don't forget to bring plenty of water, warm clothes, and raingear, in any season.

Drive to Chittenden Road, located on the Tower–Canyon Road about 5 miles north of Dunraven Pass (8.5 miles south of Tower

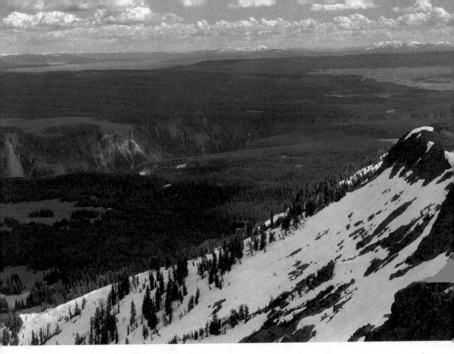

View south from Mount Washburn

Junction and 8.5 miles north of Canyon Village). Drive about 1.2 miles on the Chittenden Road to its upper parking area. Early in the season, this section of road may be closed, and cyclists must park in the lower parking area, adding over 2 miles to the trip. (See map on p. 93.)

Tourists once drove to the top of Mount Washburn. Now, thankfully, only cyclists and hikers can use the Chittenden Road. This road was named for Hiram Chittenden, an innovative road engineer in Yellowstone and its first historian.

The road alternately passes stretches of severely burnt forest and jubilantly flowered meadows. Standing snags welcome shockingly blue mountain bluebirds. Look for them among the bare, white branches. Long views from Chittenden Road reveal the mosaic pattern of the 1988 burns. Patches of bare trees stand beside healthy green stands. Shifting winds, differences in moisture levels, and variance in tree size and distribution all affected the path and severity of the burn.

Follow the road's long, loopy switchbacks. As you near the summit, watch for the mountain's small herd of bighorn sheep, present only during the summer. As described in Trip 12, a fire lookout station is located on the summit. Visitors can enter the lower level to escape the often bitter winds and inclement weather that frequents the 10,000-foot peak. For more detailed information on Mount Washburn and its incredible views, see Trip 12.

To return to the trailhead, cyclists must go back on the Chittenden Road. Do not take the road heading back to Dunraven Pass, as that is strictly for hikers.

Seven-Mile Hole

DIFFICULTY: strenuous
DISTANCE: 5.5 miles one way
USAGE: moderate
STARTING ELEVATION: 7,800 feet; elevation loss, 1,400 feet
SEASON: late May through early October
Maps: USGS 7.5-minute Mount Washburn and Canyon Village, WY

This difficult trail takes hikers to the bottom of Yellowstone's Grand Canyon, 7 miles downstream of the canyon's Lower Falls and a thousand feet beneath its gorgeous yellow cliffs. Be forewarned that climbing out of the canyon is very demanding, especially on a warm summer day. For those not up to this challenge, the trail's first 1.2 miles offer a shady, mostly level walk along the canyon's north rim, affording good views and an escape from crowded observation points.

The trail begins at a glacial boulder, a 500-ton erratic dropped from a glacier moving through this area 15,000 years ago. (The gneiss is estimated to be more than 600 million years old.) To find the boulder, drive southeast from Canyon Village on the North Rim Drive (one way) about 0.75 mile, and then turn left on a two-way road heading east. Drive 0.5 mile and watch for the boulder on the left (north) side of the road. Park along the road next to the boulder.

The trail leads east through a lodgepole pine forest. The

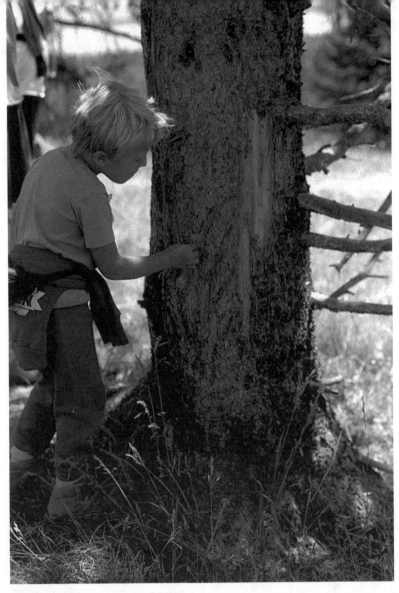

Boy examining tree clawed by bear

ground cover is thick with grouse whortleberry, a small, reddish purple berry with tiny elliptical leaves. The tasty berries provide hikers, birds, and bears with a delicious late summer snack.

The trail parallels the rim of the canyon. Short spur trails to the rim provide excellent views. While at the canyon's edge, scan the rock pinnacles for osprey nests, identifiable as large clumps

of mud, sticks, and debris atop the columns. Osprey build nests as large as 5 feet in diameter. Sharp eyes might also spy the handsome brown-and-white hawks. The wings of an osprey are dark brown and its head white, with a distinctive black band across its eyes. Osprey can dive over 100 feet, plunging feet-first into the water, emerging with a fish securely clasped in its talons. The osprey always turns the fish to face forward, taking advantage of aerodynamics as it flies to its nest or perch to eat.

After only 1.2 miles, look for a well-trod spur trail to your right. Follow that trail to an overlook of Silver Cord Cascade. The cascade's thin ribbon of water drops 1,300 feet from the opposite side of the canyon, making it the highest cascade in Yellowstone. Those seeking only an easy walk should return to the main trail and go back to the trailhead at this point.

Those heading to Seven-Mile Hole continue northeast. The trail soon veers north, leaving the canyon rim. Arrive at a trail junction with the Howard Eaton Trail and stay right (north). Head through lodgepole forest for approximately 1.3 miles. The trail begins to descend steeply. After crossing a bridge over a stream, arrive at a fork in the trail. To the left is the Mount Washburn Trail. Take the right fork (heading northeast) to Seven-Mile Hole.

The trail initially courses lazily through thick and peaceful forest and then suddenly arrives at the canyon rim. Dark pine boughs frame the immense orange-and-white canyon walls. Below, the green Yellowstone River runs white with frothy rapids. Steam rises from areas of thermal activity. The trail descends with seriousness.

Follow the steep switchbacks with care. Loose, gravelly soil provides poor footing. Pass steaming fumaroles, small meadows, and stands of low-lying juniper trees. Juniper trees are easily recognized by their hard, green berrylike cones that are used as flavoring for gin. Crush one in your hand to detect its familiar scent. Native Americans ate juniper berries and, in times of scarcity, also consumed the tree's inner bark.

Pass signs for campsites and look for orange metal blazes marking the trail. The air becomes noticeably cooler and moister as you approach the river. Finally at the river's edge, at the bottom of the canyon, enjoy a well-deserved rest. Pull out a fishing pole, binoculars, or picnic and contemplate the peacefulness and wonder of this extraordinary space. To return, retrace your steps, allowing plenty of time for the tough trek up.

15

Lookout Point to Red Rock Point

DIFFICULTY: easy
DISTANCE: 0.4 mile one way
USAGE: high
STARTING ELEVATION: 7,840 feet; elevation loss,
   500 feet
SEASON: late May to early October
MAP: USGS 7.5-minute Canyon Village, WY

For fabulous views of Yellowstone Canyon's Lower Falls, hike down to Red Rock Point from Lookout Point. After several switchbacks, a wooden staircase leads hikers to a viewing platform

Climbing the stairs from Red Rock Point

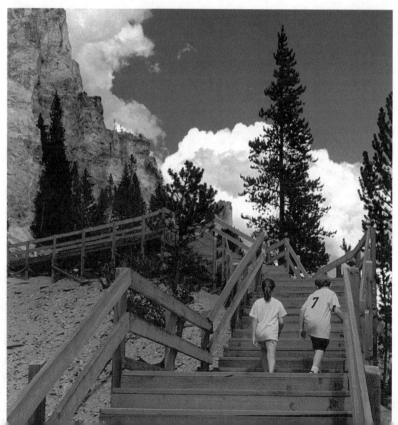

overlooking the falls. It's an impressive reward for a short, albeit steep, walk.

From Canyon Junction, drive west 1.5 miles on the one-way North Rim Drive to Lookout Point, and park in the well-marked parking area.

Before you descend to Red Rock Point, visit the Lookout Point viewing platform. As well as gaining an awesome view, sharp eyes can spy three osprey nests. Look for huge, bushel-shaped twig nests atop the rock pillars. From the viewpoint, look across the canyon to two pillars rising from the opposite side: one directly across, the other slightly to the left. A nest is also visible to the left of the viewpoint on the near side of the canyon. With binoculars, you may even see the birds or their young within the nests. Osprey mate for life and produce two or three offspring each year.

Next, descend on the steep path leading to Red Rock Point. The volume of water pouring through the narrow canyon is awesome. In spring, snowmelt swells its volume to 64,000 gallons per minute. At that rate, an Olympic-size swimming pool could be filled in a mere 30 seconds! This wild torrent of water continues to deepen the canyon by wearing away the soft volcanic rock. Since the last glaciers moved through this area 10,000 years ago, the river has dropped 50 feet.

The Lower Falls is 308 feet high, about three times the height of Niagara Falls. It was Niagara's honky-tonk commercial development in the 1870s that prompted the awestruck members of Yellowstone's early expeditions to argue so persuasively for establishment of this park. Imagine, if you can, a power plant utilizing the immense hydropower of the Yellowstone River, accompanied by the smokestacks of factories employing this electricity, joined by motels lining the North Rim Drive offering honeymoon suites, waterbeds, and cable TV. We must be thankful for the foresight of the early conservationists! The Yellowstone River remains the longest undammed river in the continental United States.

For an even more dramatic view of the Lower Falls, try the Brink of Lower Falls Trail (Trip 16).

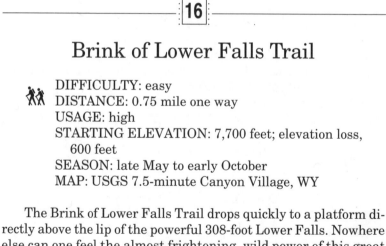

16

Brink of Lower Falls Trail

DIFFICULTY: easy
DISTANCE: 0.75 mile one way
USAGE: high
STARTING ELEVATION: 7,700 feet; elevation loss, 600 feet
SEASON: late May to early October
MAP: USGS 7.5-minute Canyon Village, WY

The Brink of Lower Falls Trail drops quickly to a platform directly above the lip of the powerful 308-foot Lower Falls. Nowhere else can one feel the almost frightening, wild power of this great rushing waterfall. The raw immediacy of its racing water and the thunder of its falling torrents impresses the most weary sightseer. If you have time for only one stop along the canyon, try this short hike.

From Canyon Junction, drive east and then south along the one-way North Rim Drive to a large, well-marked parking area located at its southern end. This is the last parking lot before the drive merges with the Canyon–Fishing Bridge Road. Don't mistake this trail for the Brink of (Upper) Falls Trail located farther south on the Canyon–Fishing Bridge Road (see map, page 102).

The trail switchbacks down steeply losing 600 feet in only 0.75 mile. If hiking in spring or fall, watch for icy conditions that make this trail dangerous and slick. At the brink of the falls, keep a close eye on youngsters. The canyon has been the site of several tragic deaths.

Hikers should take their time on the return ascent, especially those not used to high-altitude hiking. If the kids are up for another close-up view of the falls, try Uncle Tom's Trail on the south rim (Trip 18).

--------------------------------- 17 ---------------------------------

Clear Lake Loop

DIFFICULTY: moderate
DISTANCE: 3.75 miles round trip (add 3.1 miles for Ribbon Lake detour)
USAGE: moderate
STARTING ELEVATION: 7,700 feet; elevation gain, 120 feet
SEASON: late May through early October
MAP: USGS 7.5-minute Canyon Village, WY

Don't miss this easy, but extraordinary, gem of a hike. The trail offers awesome canyon views, a variety of thermal features, two lovely lakes, and meadows filled with flowers (and often wildlife). Early or late in the day, especially in the spring or fall, hikers may see elk, bison, or mule deer. Bears also frequent the area, particularly early and late in the season. For the most beautiful canyon views, hike this trail late in the afternoon.

Drive south from Canyon Junction 2.2 miles to the Chittenden Bridge. Turn left and drive over the bridge onto Artist Point Road.

Drive approximately 0.5 mile to a large parking lot signed for Uncle Tom's Trail. As you enter the lot, note the trailhead for Clear Lake located on your right. Before setting out, pick up a NPS brochure describing the canyon area at a dispenser near the start of Uncle Tom's Trail.

The Clear Lake Trail immediately takes you south across Artist Point Road and into open meadows. Views to the north include Mount Washburn (10,243 feet). Watch for soaring red-tailed hawks hunting for meadow rodents. Throughout the meadow grows a scraggly shrub, called rabbitbrush, whose stems and leaves are covered with fine, whitish hairs. Wildlife, especially rabbits, enjoy its leaves and foliage. Small mammals also use the shrub for cover. Depending on the season, a variety of flowers graces the meadow. In early summer, the display is at its finest. Watch for pink shooting stars, yellow arrowleaf balsamroot, and white sego lilies.

Gently observing a nest (Please do not remove natural objects.)

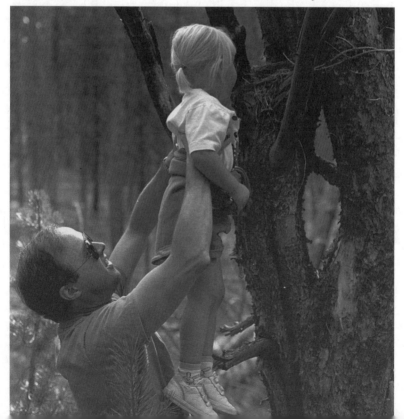

After 0.9 mile, arrive at a trail junction with the Wapiti Lake Trail. Take the left (northeast) fork. In 0.1 mile, arrive at Clear Lake. The large, beautiful green lake is a perfect place for a picnic, *if* the winds are cooperating. Thermal features on the north side of the lake emit a sulphurous odor that some may find objectionable.

The trail continues along the east side of Clear Lake. As you pass the lake, the odor of sulphur increases until you arrive at a particularly amusing mud pot. Stand back to avoid the splattering mud. Stay on the trail across a rocky area, a virtual garden of small thermal features. Look for bubbling hot springs, hissing steam vents covered with green and yellow algae, and more odorous mud pots. Do not approach any thermal feature, as the surrounding crust may be thin.

One half mile from Clear Lake, arrive at a trail junction. Bear left for Lily Pad Lake. The trail to the right leads to Ribbon Lake in 1.3 miles. The trail to Ribbon Lake takes you through pleasant lodgepole forest to a series of lakes. If you choose to visit the Ribbon Lake area (the detour adds 3.1 miles to the hike), be sure to follow the Ribbon Lake Trail northeast to the lake's outlet. Cross the outlet and head north to the rim of the canyon. As well as gaining beautiful canyon views, you'll be at the head of Silver Cord Cascade, which plunges over 1,000 feet to the Yellowstone River. (For another view of the cascade, see Trip 14.) To return, retrace your steps along the Ribbon Lake Trail. Backpacking families will find a nice campsite at Ribbon Lake.

For those hiking the shorter loop, stay left to reach well-named Lily Pad Lake. The pond is covered with pond lilies, quite a pretty sight when the large yellow flowers are blooming. Native Americans enjoyed the seeds of the pond lily roasted, and they are reputed to taste like popcorn. Today they are relished by waterfowl. Watch also for muskrat who feed on the lily's submerged rootstalks.

The roar of the Yellowstone River is audible at Lily Pad Lake, for the canyon is only 0.1 mile to the north. Follow the trail along the west side of the lake via sandy switchbacks to the canyon rim. At the rim, the view is unequaled. The canyon's colors are almost shocking in their intensity, particularly late in the day. The intense pinks, oranges, and yellows of the canyon's walls were created when heat from thermal activity altered the normally brownish rhyolite rock.

Canyon enthusiasts can indulge in another detour by hiking 0.5

mile northeast along the rim to Point Sublime. The walk affords more magnificent canyon views, usually with few other hikers. The scenery is staggeringly beautiful. Pay attention to youngsters on these stretches, as the trail drops off quite steeply in places.

To head back toward the trailhead, turn left toward Artist Point (0.5 mile to the southwest). The remainder of the hike follows the canyon's south rim. In the canyon, watch for brown-and-white osprey and jet black ravens. Osprey build huge nests atop the canyon's rock pinnacles. Two nests are visible from Artist Point Lookout. Ravens hide nests in holes in the canyon walls.

From Artist Point, the South Rim Trail continues southwest about 1 mile to Uncle Tom's Parking Area. The mostly paved path alternates between canyon views and shady lodgepole forest. Before you reach Uncle Tom's Parking Area, arrive at a trail junction with Uncle Tom's Trail. To view (and feel!) the Lower Falls from an observation platform dramatically constructed 500 feet below the canyon rim, turn right at the junction (for a full description, see Trip 18).

To return directly to the trailhead, keep left. At a second trail junction just 0.1 mile farther, again stay left to ascend to the parking area.

18

Uncle Tom's Trail

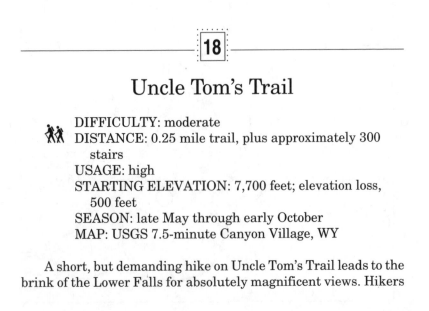

DIFFICULTY: moderate
DISTANCE: 0.25 mile trail, plus approximately 300 stairs
USAGE: high
STARTING ELEVATION: 7,700 feet; elevation loss, 500 feet
SEASON: late May through early October
MAP: USGS 7.5-minute Canyon Village, WY

A short, but demanding hike on Uncle Tom's Trail leads to the brink of the Lower Falls for absolutely magnificent views. Hikers descend over 500 feet on steel platforms bolted to the canyon wall. This trail is often crowded, so arrive in the early morning for solitude. To view a rainbow in the spray, try late morning or early afternoon. Follow the directions in Trip 17 to reach Uncle Tom's Parking Area and Trailhead.

This trail was named for Tom Richardson, who, in 1903, built a "trail" at this location where hikers lowered themselves into the canyon on rope ladders. Today hikers descend on over three hundred steel stairs. Nevertheless, this trail can still be very dangerous. Be extremely careful when ice coats the stairs, as may occur in spring, fall, or early morning in any season.

Follow the clearly marked path from the parking lot. At the first junction, turn right. Shortly, arrive at a second junction and turn left. Immediately, meet another fork and stay right. To the left is a viewpoint over the Lower Falls; stay right to descend directly into the canyon.

Follow the stairs, descending along the moist canyon wall. At the bottom, the roar of the water is intense. In spring and early summer when the river is full of snowmelt, the platform is doused with spray. In spring, a glorious 64,000 gallons of water per second race over the falls. At times of low water, this volume is reduced to 5,000 gallons per second.

How were these awesome falls created? In simple terms, the Yellowstone River flows through an ancient geyser basin beginning at the Upper Falls. The river was able to erode this basin to a deep canyon because the hot, acidic water of thermal features weakened the underlying rock. Where the rock was thermally altered (and therefore softened), the river was able to carve it away. The Upper and Lower falls developed in the transition zone where sections of underlying rock were not affected by thermal activity. These shelves of rock were stronger and therefore resistant to the eroding force of the flowing water. While the rock above and below it has fallen away, water tumbles over the enduring rock shelf of the Lower Falls.

If you think Uncle Tom's man-made stairway is too intrusive in a place of such natural grandeur, be thankful that commercial interests were prevented in the 1890s from installing an elevator at the Lower Falls! Owen Wister, author of *The Virginian*, wrote of the narrowly defeated elevator proposal, "Politics was behind it, as usual. To put a lot of machinery by those Falls at the head of the canyon, where the sublime merges with the exquisite, and which alone is worth crossing the continent to see, would have been an outrage more abominable than the dam at Jackson Lake."

If youngsters balk at climbing back up the gazillion stairs, try this: have each child guess how many steps there are, and then count them on the way back up. (The answer is 328; be prepared with suitable rewards!)

19

Artist Paint Pots Trail

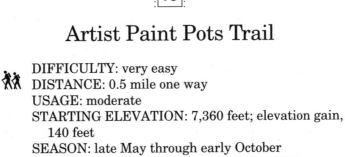

DIFFICULTY: very easy
DISTANCE: 0.5 mile one way
USAGE: moderate
STARTING ELEVATION: 7,360 feet; elevation gain,
    140 feet
SEASON: late May through early October
MAP: USGS 7.5-minute Norris Junction, WY

Leave the crowds at Gibbon Meadows for a delightfully short hike to fascinating thermal features starkly set in a burned forest. Youngsters will be captivated by strange-colored pools and a huge, spitting, burping mud pot. In spring and fall, elk are plentiful along the trail.

From Norris, drive 4.2 miles south on the Norris–Madison Road to the trailhead on the road's east side, signed for "Artist Paint Pots Trail." From Madison, drive 9.8 miles north on the Norris–Madison Road to the trailhead.

Most of the tourist activity in the area is directed toward Gibbon Meadows on the west side of the road, where elk and bison graze year round along the Gibbon River. The number of animals visible in the meadow increases significantly from September through May. Gibbon Meadows and Elk Park (just a few miles north) are the wintering grounds for thousands of elk in Yellowstone's Gibbon–Madison–Firehole herd.

The trail to the paint pots begins on a boardwalk then heads east (left) along the base of a charred hillside. This area was extensively burned in 1988 by the North Fork Fire, the largest fire of that extraordinary summer. Happily, regrowth is apparent along the trail. In fact, young hikers born in late 1988 and 1989 find the young lodgepoles especially interesting, for they can measure the progress of a small forest just their age!

Along the hillside in late summer, watch for grouse whortleberries, a delicious relative of the blueberry with very delicate, egg-shaped leaves. These sweet, reddish purple berries were much enjoyed by Native Americans and today are relished by wildlife and hungry hikers. Hugging the ground also are small woodland strawberries, another particularly tasty treat. Above you, in the

Roiling mudpot on Artist Paint Pots Trail

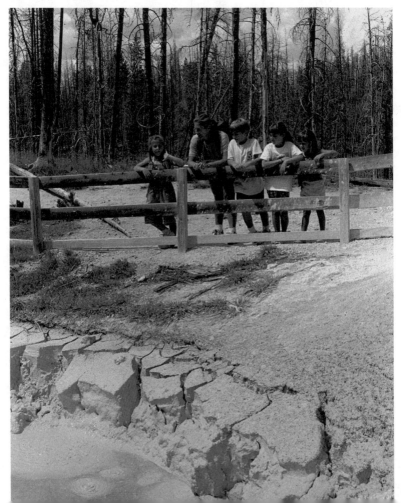

branches of the fir and lodgepole, hang bright green lichen. In the winter when forage is scarce, the lichen is a nutritious food for elk and mule deer.

As you walk among the lodgepole pine, notice the many slender trees whose bark has been scraped off. This is the work of bull elk who use the trees to remove velvet from their antlers. Fuzzy "velvet" covers the elk's fast-growing antlers throughout the summer. Blood vessels within the velvet nourish the growing antler bone. Elk antlers grow extremely fast, as much as an inch a day! Full-grown racks of a mature bull can reach 5 feet across and weigh 40 pounds. When the antlers cease growing, the elk rubs off the velvet by using the sides of young lodgepoles. Observant visitors may spy a bull "jousting" with a lodgepole, his velvet hanging like a decrepit rag from beautiful, burnished antlers.

After 0.2 mile, reach a trail junction. Stay to the left and regain the boardwalk. The rumbling, steam, and smell of the thermal area are now evident. Pass the first of the "paint pots," a milky blue pool, followed by a chalky white pot. Iron-oxide minerals give the pools their unusual colors. Yellow, brown, and orange algae expand the palette.

Cross a bridge over a hot spring, and then rise with the trail as it loops back in a westerly direction. The views improve with the elevation gain. Below are pools of various colors, easily visible in the fire-cleared landscape. Beyond on the northern horizon are the Gallatin Mountains.

On the upper loop, mud pots and hot springs are plentiful. The trail's highlight for most children is the large mud pot at the west end of the upper loop. Behind a splattered wooden corral, a huge belching, spitting mud pot entertains noisily. Mud is routinely flung 10 feet in the air. On angry days, visitors have to stand a few feet behind the railing.

What is causing this strange phenomenon? Mud pots are hot springs with a limited water supply. Boiling water beneath the surface produces sulfuric acid. Because of the scarcity of water, the acid cannot be washed away. This acid dissolves some of the rock with which it comes in contact, creating a thick, sticky clay. The burping and bubbling of the mud pots is produced by steam and gas vapors rising and escaping through the mud.

From the mud pot, the trail re-enters the lodgepole forest and heads downhill rather steeply. At the bottom of the hill, bear left to return to the trailhead.

20

Two Ribbons Trail

DIFFICULTY: very easy; handicapped accessible
according to federal standards
DISTANCE: 0.75 mile round trip
USAGE: low
STARTING ELEVATION: 6,700 feet; no elevation gain
SEASON: mid-May to early October
MAP: USGS 7.5-minute West Yellowstone, WY

The Two Ribbons Trail provides a handicapped-accessible boardwalk over riverbank burned by the 1988 fire. Like the Children's Fire Trail (Trip 6), the Two Ribbons Trail is an intimate introduction to fire ecology. It is also a pleasant stroll among sculptural snags, vivid flowers, and the sparkling Madison River.

From Yellowstone's West Entrance, drive 3 miles east on the West Entrance–Madison Road to a turnout (11 miles west of Madison Junction) on the left (north) side of the road. There are two turnouts, you may begin the hike at either end. The following description is written for those beginning at the easternmost turnout.

The boardwalk heads immediately to the edge of the Madison River. This river is one of the most highly prized trout streams in North America. Trout favor its clear waters and ample gravel spawning beds. But the real secret of the Madison is its temperature. Thermal runoff from nearby hot springs keeps the Madison relatively warm year-round. Hot springs also add minerals to the water which promote the growth of aquatic plants, that in turn attract insects (food for the trout).

In midsummer the flowers are striking along the boardwalk. Blackened snags contrast pleasingly with the magenta fireweed. Fireweed (also called "blooming Sally") is one of the first plants to colonize burned areas. Its parachuting seeds (with long hairs that catch the wind) quickly spread the plants over wide areas. Fireweed helps hold and enrich scorched soil so that a variety of plants, shrubs, and trees can follow. Fireweed is also a valuable food source, especially for elk. Before the fireweed blooms, lavender lupine, buckwheat, and a variety of yellow composites add color to the area.

Already a great many young lodgepole are thriving along the boardwalk. Prior to 1988, this forest was not a healthy one. Many of its pines were killed by pine bark beetles. When the North Fork fire swept the area, these dead and dying trees, lacking the moisture of healthy pines, went up like match sticks. Consequently the fire actually hastened a rebirth. Without fire, a fallen lodgepole can take a century to decompose. After the fire, valuable soil nutrients were released from standing snags and downed trees in a fraction of the time.

As you continue west on the boardwalk, stay to the right and enter a stand of trees spared by the fire. This is characteristic of most of the burned areas of the park. Shifting winds and tree conditions caused the fire to burn in patches rather than wreaking total destruction.

Look down to find large, round patties by the boardwalk. These were left by bison, who are frequently seen in the meadows along the Madison River. The banks of the Madison also provide excellent year-round habitat for elk, trumpeter swans, and occasional moose.

From the boardwalk, there are good views of the Gallatin Range to the north and west. To the immediate southeast, Mount Haynes rises to 8,235 feet. Follow the boardwalk as it loops around closer to the road and returns you to the trailhead.

Jackson Lake, Grand Teton National Park

CHAPTER

4

South Yellowstone

The southern half of Yellowstone National Park contains some of its most famous sights, including the Upper, Middle, and Lower Geyser basins and lovely Yellowstone Lake. Visitors can find hiking trails rich in diversity, three fine biking trails, and a wealth of boardwalks from which to view fascinating thermal features.

To find beauty along the shore of Yellowstone Lake, hike the trails in Trips 21 and 22. For an impressive lake overlook, try Trip 23. A picnic on the beach behind the Fishing Bridge Visitor Center can also be quite relaxing and offers a 0.5-mile stretch of sandy beach on which to stroll or cast for fish. Those wanting to explore Yellowstone Lake by boat should inquire about guided tours or charter boats at Bridge Bay Marina (see Chapter 1).

Hikers seeking thermal features can explore Biscuit Basin and a lovely cascade on Trip 25, the Old Faithful Geyser Basin on Trip 26, or a unique backcountry geyser on Trip 28. Two pretty backcountry lakes are also easily accessible, Shoshone Lake (Trip 29) and Riddle Lake (Trip 30). Backpacking families can find good sites on Trips 28 and 29.

There are some good cycling opportunities in South Yellowstone also. Cyclists can ride the bike trail at the Upper Geyser Basin (Trip 27), ride the scenic Fountain Flat Drive (Trip 24), cycle the strange and interesting Firehole Lake Drive, or take their mountain bikes to a backcountry geyser (Trip 28).

Water adventures are available as well. Hot summer days bring carloads of swimmers to the swimming hole at the end of Firehole Canyon Drive. From wading to intrepid wave riding, youngsters of all ages enjoy the natural setting and thermally warmed waters of the Firehole River. It's also an immensely popular place to picnic. Swimmers should remember, however, that diving and jumping from cliffs is strictly prohibited and unconscionably dangerous.

Visitors to South Yellowstone should stop by the Grant Visitor Center to view its fascinating fire exhibit and films. For the many interpretive talks and walks offered by the park service in this area, inquire at park visitor centers or consult the park publication *Discover Yellowstone*.

21

Pelican Creek Loop

DIFFICULTY: easy
DISTANCE: 1-mile loop
USAGE: low
STARTING ELEVATION: 7,760 feet; elevation gain, none
SEASON: July through September
MAP: USGS 7.5-minute Lake Butte, WY

On a hot summer day, Pelican Creek Loop is an excellent hike for young families. A short and shady path leads to a lovely sandy beach on Yellowstone Lake, where the water is shallow and temperate and magnificent scenery abounds. Pelican Valley, located just north of this trail, is prime grizzly habitat, so be sure to check with rangers before hiking. Closures or restrictions may apply.

Drive 0.9 mile east of the Fishing Bridge Visitor Center on the Fishing Bridge–East Entrance Road. Find the trailhead and parking pullout on the south side of the road, just west of the Pelican Creek Bridge.

Nearby Pelican Valley is one of Yellowstone's most important

Hikers making strides

habitats for grizzlies. Since 1975, the grizzly has been listed as threatened under the Endangered Species Act. In fact, Yellowstone has one of only two viable grizzly populations south of Canada. Where 100,000 grizzlies once roamed from Mexico to the Arctic in the 1800s, now only 1,000 (at best) inhabit islands of protected habitat in Wyoming and Montana. Currently the park estimates that there are about 250 grizzlies left in Yellowstone, owing to encroachments upon their habitat by development and recreational use. Consequently, hiking in Pelican Valley is restricted to day use between 9 A.M. and 7 P.M. to minimize human contact with the bears.

Follow the trail into a lush forest where it immediately forks. Head right and enter gardens of lavender lupine, magenta fireweed, white buckwheat and yarrow, blue phlox, and numerous yellow composites. Watch for mule deer sampling this colorful buffet. In late summer, you may taste too; try the wild strawberries and sweet, blue huckleberries.

In the rich, moist soil near the lake, forest succession is taking place. The older lodgepole pines are giving way to spruce and fir. The sun-loving lodgepole was the pioneer. Its dense canopy provided the shade essential to spruce and fir seedlings. When the spruce and fir mature, their branches will shut off the sun and ensure that future generations of their seedlings will thrive. Lodgepole will not return until fire, insect infestation, landslide, or other natural disturbance clears the trees and opens the land once again to the sun.

To East Entrance

Fishing Bridge-East Entrance Road

0   N◀   1

MILES

Indian Pond

Trip 22   T P

Storm Point

Marmot colony

Storm Point Nature Trail

Pelican Creek

Trip 21   Pelican Creek Loop Trail   T P

Yellowstone Lake

Yellowstone River

Fishing Bridge Visitor Center

$ Store

To Canyon Junction

Fishing Bridge Junction

Fishing Bridge-West Thumb Road

Lake Village

Trip 23

Elephant Back Mountain Trail

T P

To West Thumb

The trail soon arrives at the sandy beach. Strip off your boots and wade in the shallow water. Most of Yellowstone Lake is frigid, making swimming impossible. Most summers, the water here warms to tolerable levels because of the shallowness of this section of the lake.

On nearby rocky islands, watch for the American white pelican. White pelicans are quite large and beautiful, with snow-white feathers and a long, bright orange beak. The white pelican lives exclusively on lakes of the American West. Unfortunately, its population has suffered in recent years due to habitat loss and the thinning of its eggs from pesticide poisoning. Enjoy watching these magnificent birds, but never approach too closely. You may inadvertently drive a bird from its nest and cause it to abandon its eggs or even its young.

The trail travels a few yards to the left (west) along the beach, and then turns back into the woods. A scenic spur trail on your right brings you to the bank of Pelican Creek.

To return to the trailhead, regain the main trail and follow it to the fork in the forest, traversing first a set of boardwalks over a wet meadow. When you arrive at the junction, bear right to reach your car.

Storm Point Nature Trail Loop

DIFFICULTY: moderate
DISTANCE: 3- to 5-mile loop
USAGE: moderate
STARTING ELEVATION: 7,800 feet; elevation gain, 50 feet
SEASON: July through September (check for trail closings)
MAP: USGS 7.5-minute Lake Butte, WY

The trail to Storm Point is especially delightful. It covers beautiful and varied terrain, visiting meadows, forests, ponds, and a stunning beach. It also provides excellent opportunities to see wildlife. This hike traverses prime grizzly territory, so hikers must check with rangers for closures or restrictions prior to departure. Because of bear activity, it is recommended that the trail be used by parties of four or more.

From Fishing Bridge Junction, drive east 3 miles on the Fishing Bridge–East Entrance Road to the Storm Point Trailhead on the right (south) side of the road (see map, page 118).

The trail begins in a pretty meadow west of Indian Pond, a favorite camping site for Native Americans. In 1880 numerous stone tools, brush horse corrals, and human shelters were found near the pond. Recently a perfectly preserved tepee ring was also discovered nearby. Indian Pond lies in an ancient volcanic crater, created by a steam explosion. Its circular shape and high embankments are clues to its violent origin. In the pond, there's a small population of cutthroat trout. Watch also for Canada geese and Barrow's goldeneye ducks. The male goldeneye has a purple head, black-and-white body, white crescents in front of its eyes, and bright orange feet.

The trail continues south past the pond. At the first fork, stay left, continuing south. As you pass mature lodgepole pines, check for signs of bear. Grizzlies rub their massive backs against the trees and often leave bits of fur in the bark or on the exposed

Yellowstone Lake, near Storm Point

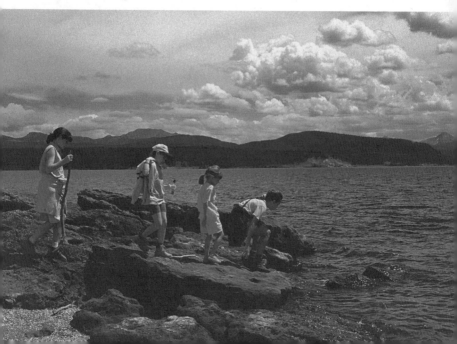

sap. Further up the trunk look for narrow, vertical cuts. These were likely made by a grizzly's long, curved claws. Grizzly claws were prized by Native Americans and were worn as a sign of bravery. Awesome specimens can be seen at the Indian Museum in Colter Bay and at the Jackson Hole Museum in Jackson.

Bison also leave their mark on mature lodgepole. They rub their massive heads and horns against the trees, removing large patches of bark. You may also find their hair matted in the sap of the debarked trees. Both males and females have horns that are never shed, composed of tightly compacted hair over a core of bone. Another sign of bison is a "wallow," a shallow depression in the ground where a bison has rolled around on its back.

Follow the trail to the beautiful and dramatically sculptured shore of Yellowstone Lake. There is plenty of beach to explore and rocks to climb. At the beach, look for tracks in the sand. Grizzly bear tracks can be identified by their large size (their hind feet may be a foot long!) and the claw marks in front of each toe.

Storm Point was named for the tremendous waves and wind that regularly batter the point. The prevailing winds on Yellowstone Lake blow from the southwest, bringing with them severe weather. The winds tend to build in the afternoon, so plan your outing accordingly. While at the lake, watch for graceful white pelicans, goldeneye ducks, and osprey.

The trail heads west above the lakeshore. In this area, watch for yellow-bellied marmots. On clear days, they are likely to be sunning themselves on the rock outcroppings. Marmots, a relative of the eastern woodchuck, spend their summer days lazily munching the park's greenery. They must build up a thick layer of fat to last them through their long winter hibernation. Please do not feed these roly-poly beggars; nature supplies them nutritionally with all that they need.

After a short stroll along the lake, the trail turns north (right) into the forest. Before entering the woods, take a short and beautiful side trip farther west along the lakeshore. Just continue along the shore for more views of striking Storm Point and a variety of waterfowl. Watch for moose in the wetlands to the right of the trail. To return to the Storm Point Trail, just retrace your steps to the point where the trail turns into the forest.

Enter the dense lodgepole forest. This type of lodgepole stand is called a "doghair" forest, for the trees are "as thick as the hair on a dog's back." Another way to explain this to youngsters is to ask them to imagine how fur looks to a flea on a dog. A doghair forest is created when trees grow so close together that the sun is unable to reach a tree's lower branches. Consequently, the lower branches lose their needles, die, and fall off, leaving a forest of bare trunks. Make lots of noise as you hike, for bears often retreat to the forest during the day to rest. If a bear should hear you, it is likely to move away to avoid an encounter. In August, don't miss the plentiful whortleberries and wild strawberries growing on the forest floor.

Finally the trail leaves the woods, crosses a creek, and arrives in an open meadow. In the meadow grows yampah, or squaw potato, a plant whose plump roots are much loved by grizzlies. The grizzlies dig them up with their long claws, which they can move independently like fingers. Yampah tastes a little like carrot and was a staple of Native Americans and mountain men. Yampah sports clusters of small, white, five-petaled flowers arranged in umbels and has slender, fernlike leaves. It grows 1 to 3 feet tall and blooms in July and August.

The trail loops back to a junction near Indian Pond. At the junction, head left (north) to return to the trailhead.

23

Elephant Back Mountain Loop

DIFFICULTY: moderate
DISTANCE: 3.5-mile loop
USAGE: moderate
STARTING ELEVATION: 7,800 feet; elevation gain, 750 feet
SEASON: late June through September
MAP: USGS 7.5-minute Lake Butte, WY

This steep trail climbs through dense forest to an excellent view of Yellowstone Lake. Youngsters may, however, find the trail tough and a bit monotonous. Also, those seeking a pristine view will be disappointed to see the park's development so obvious along the lakeshore. Despite these drawbacks, the vista from the summit is

Yellowstone Lake from Elephant Back Mountain

still gorgeous. This trail is not recommended for spring hiking, since grizzlies are frequently sighted in the area in May and June.

Drive about 1 mile south from the Fishing Bridge Junction on the Fishing Bridge–West Thumb Road. The trailhead is on the west side of the road (for map, see page 118). Park along the roadside.

The trail parallels the road briefly, and then turns westward to head into lodgepole forest. The forest is pleasant, with a green undergrowth of grass and flowers. For a refreshing treat, look for tiny wild strawberries in late summer. The trail soon climbs moderately. At a fork in the trail, take the left path and switchback up, sometimes steeply, to the top of the mountain.

At the top there are excellent picnic spots with panoramic views. Below you is magnificent Yellowstone Lake, measuring 20 by 14 miles, with islands, beautiful bays, and a gorgeous undulating shoreline. Don't miss viewing the lake at sunrise and sunset when the water's still surface shares the brilliant colors of the sky and mountains.

At the summit, a young hiking companion asked, upon seeing the sprawling hotel/hospital/lodge complex below, "When are we going back to the park?" His idea of Yellowstone was forests, not parking lots; bears, not buildings. I directed his gaze south to the Red Mountains and east to the snow-capped Absarokas, but deep down, I felt his question was wise and telling.

To return to the trailhead, follow the loop trail northeast. The trail descends via switchbacks, and then swings southwest to meet the main trail. At the junction, keep left to reach the trailhead.

:24:

Fountain Flat Road and Fairy Falls

DIFFICULTY: easy
DISTANCE: 5 miles one way via bike (plus 1.6 miles one-way hike)
USAGE: moderate
STARTING ELEVATION: 7,200 feet; elevation gain, 50 feet
SEASON: mid-May to early October
MAP: USGS 7.5-minute Lower Geyser Basin, WY

Cyclists will enjoy riding through open meadows and burned forest along the scenic Firehole River to Midway Geyser Basin. The first 1.6 miles are on paved road, which you share with car traffic for the first 0.9 mile. In 1996, the park plans to close Fountain Flat Road to cars after this point, which will significantly improve this ride. At about 4 miles from the trailhead, cyclists can leave their bikes and take a short (1.6 mile) hike to pretty Fairy Falls. To have the road to yourself, begin this ride early in the day.

To reach Fountain Flat Road, drive 10 miles north of Old Faithful on the Old Faithful–Madison Road or drive 6 miles south of Madison. Turn southwest onto Fountain Flat Road. There is parking just across the bridge at the Nez Perce Creek Picnic Area. If you want to avoid all car traffic, drive on Fountain Flat Road until you reach the locked gate.

From the Nez Perce Creek Picnic Area, ride south along the Firehole River. The meadows flanking the river are home to elk, bison, coyote, and sandhill cranes. The warmth of the river keeps the mammals here year round. In 1850, mountain man and raconteur Jim Bridger reported that the Firehole River "flowed so fast down the side of the hill that the friction of the water against the rocks, heated the rocks." Though this is obviously a tall tale, hot

Girls with post-fire lodgepole pine

springs beneath the riverbed do heat the river bottom in many places. For example, at 1 mile, pass Ojo Caliente Spring, a fine, crested hot spring just west of the road. Hot springs like Ojo Caliente can raise the river temperature a toasty 20 degrees. Cross the river on a narrow bridge. The waters are rich with cunning brown, rainbow, and brook trout.

After the bridge, the Firehole slips out of sight, and you proceed through forest burned by the 1988 North Fork Fire. It was this blaze that swept voraciously southeast to nearly consume the historic Old Faithful Inn. Miraculously, winds shifted just in time to save the magnificent structure.

At 1.6 miles, the dirt road begins. Pass the junction with the first trail to Fairy Falls and a lake on your left. At a little over 3 miles, arrive at Goose and Feather lakes and the end of the old automobile road. This is an excellent place for a rest stop. The Firehole River winds scenically below you. The water here is fairly warm, so you may want to soothe your feet at the river's edge. Swimming in the river, however, is discouraged by the NPS.

Resume your ride on the road beyond the gate, traveling south. After 0.6 mile, the level road brings you to the junction with the second trail to Fairy Falls. If time allows, hike the 1.6-mile trail to the 200-foot-high falls (about 1 hour round-trip, no bicycles allowed). The easy, mostly level trail travels west through badly burned forest to the high, feathery falls. In midsummer, the forest is colorful with flowers and the occasional mountain bluebird. Imperial Geyser, just 0.7 mile farther on the well-marked trail, has unfortunately ceased erupting.

From the Fairy Falls Trailhead, the road continues south, and then curves southeast along the edge of the Midway Geyser Basin. At the steel bridge across the Firehole River, turn around and ride back to your car.

Mystic Falls Loop

DIFFICULTY: moderate
DISTANCE: 3.2-mile loop
USAGE: moderate
STARTING ELEVATION: 7,274 feet; elevation gain, 420 feet
SEASON: late May to early October
MAP: USGS 7.5-minute Old Faithful, WY

Hike a diverse and pleasant trail to 70-foot Mystic Falls. Enjoy fine forest walking, a clear rushing stream, some boulder-hopping, cascade viewing, and a superb overlook of the Upper Geyser Basin. In spring and fall, you may encounter bison, elk, and even moose along the trail. For a special treat, leave the trailhead 45 to 60 minutes before the estimated eruption of Old Faithful or Castle geysers, and you'll have a fabulous view from the scenic overlook (about 1.7 miles from the trailhead).

Drive to Biscuit Basin, located 2 miles north of the Old Faithful cloverleaf on the West Thumb–Madison Road and park in Biscuit Basin's large parking lot. Before you leave the parking lot, take note of the steam rising from vents in the asphalt. You are standing in the crater of an immense volcano, created by an eruption 600,000 years ago. The volcano's fiery remains still smolder beneath your feet. Its thermal power fuels the largest collection of hot springs, geysers, and mud pots known on earth.

Cross the Firehole River (trout are often visible from the bridge) and walk on the boardwalk to beautiful Sapphire Pool.

Billowing clouds of steam waft from its jewel blue depths. Sapphire Pool was once edged with biscuit-shaped rock formations, but a major earthquake in 1959 caused the pool to erupt violently, knocking off all of the "biscuits."

To find the trailhead, continue west to the end of the boardwalk. Across from tumultuous Avoca Spring, the trail begins. This area was badly burned by the 1988 North Fork Fire. In the forest today, regrowth is evident everywhere, with abundant young lodgepole, bright pink fireweed, and lavender lupine. The abundance of snags (standing dead trees) is good news for bluebirds, woodpeckers, and other insect-loving, cavity-nesting birds.

After 0.6 mile, arrive at a trail junction with the trail to the overlook. Descend to the left. In just 0.1 mile, arrive at a junction with the Summit Lake Trail. Head right for Mystic Falls. The trail follows the Little Firehole River as it approaches the falls. The moisture of the vegetation near the riverbanks spared most of the trees from the fire, though you have only to look on the river's opposite bank to see the devastation. Relish the green garden of pines and flowers growing lushly along this stretch of trail, accompanied by the sparkling water of the Little Firehole.

Prominent among the many flowers is the beautiful fringed gentian, Yellowstone's official flower. The gentian is easily recognized by its deep purple, fringed petals. In early summer these slopes are also covered by arrowleaf balsamroot, a bright yellow composite whose leaves are shaped like arrowheads. Elk and mule deer enjoy the balsamroot's tender shoots.

Arrive at Mystic Falls, just 1 mile from the trailhead. The small, tiered cascade is delightfully situated for exploration. For good views, descend (carefully) to the river. Watch for hot springs feeding into the river at the base of the falls. To observe from above, follow the switchbacks. A steep spur trail to the left descends dramatically to the lip of the falls. This maneuver requires the utmost care, and children should be watched diligently.

In the rocky area around the falls, watch and listen for yellow-bellied marmots, also called "whistle pigs" for the high-pitched sound they emit as a warning to fellow marmots. Marmots resemble rotund groundhogs, with small, fur-covered ears, golden bellies, and reddish brown backs. Marmots can be seen in rocky areas from June to September.

At the top of the falls, climb briefly on switchbacks to the top of the ridge. Then head north (right) to return to Biscuit Basin via the overlook (1.7 miles). You are now traversing the edge of the Madison Plateau. Look carefully through the forest to the left for elk and possibly moose.

Arrive at the overlook and enjoy panoramic views to the east over Biscuit Basin, Black Sand Basin, and the Upper Geyser Basin, including Old Faithful. In the Upper Geyser Basin alone, there are 140 geysers within 1 square mile, nearly 20 percent of the entire earth's geysers. Add the Lower Geyser Basin, and there are more than 300 geysers and about 10,000 thermal features, more than exist in all the rest of the world combined. You can easily pick out Old Faithful in the Upper Geyser Basin by identifying the wooden buildings surrounding it.

From the overlook, the effects of the 1988 fire are dramatic. Fallen trees lie like toothpicks on the hillsides. Islands of trees relatively untouched by the fire illustrate the mosaic pattern of the burn. To return to Biscuit Basin, follow the switchbacks down the steep slope. At the trail junction at the bottom of the hill, stay left and continue east to reach the basin boardwalk.

26

Observation Point

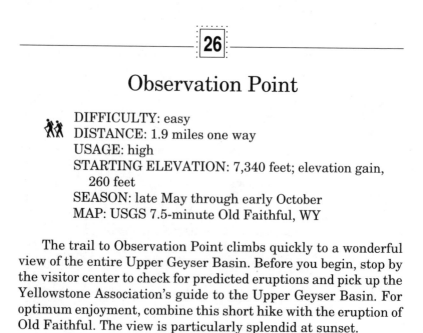

DIFFICULTY: easy
DISTANCE: 1.9 miles one way
USAGE: high
STARTING ELEVATION: 7,340 feet; elevation gain, 260 feet
SEASON: late May through early October
MAP: USGS 7.5-minute Old Faithful, WY

The trail to Observation Point climbs quickly to a wonderful view of the entire Upper Geyser Basin. Before you begin, stop by the visitor center to check for predicted eruptions and pick up the Yellowstone Association's guide to the Upper Geyser Basin. For optimum enjoyment, combine this short hike with the eruption of Old Faithful. The view is particularly splendid at sunset.

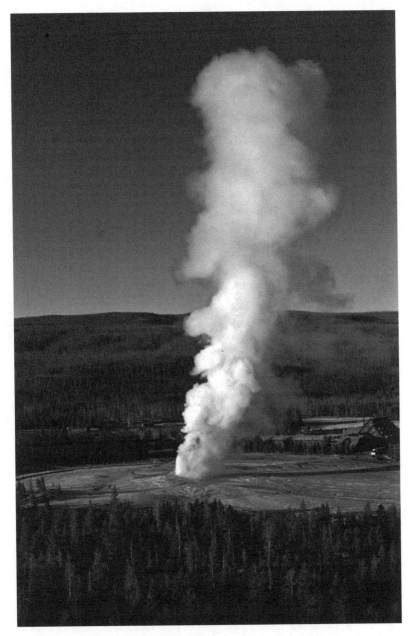

Old Faithful from Observation Point

Drive to Old Faithful, located on the West Thumb–Madison Road 17 miles north of West Thumb and 16 miles south of Madison. Follow signs for the Old Faithful Visitor Center and park in any of the large lots surrounding the complex.

From the visitor center, walk toward Old Faithful, and then head east on the paved path keeping Old Faithful on your left. Soon pass the Old Faithful Lodge and Cafeteria. Under the boardwalk in front of the lodge, you are likely to see yellow-bellied marmots. The marmots congregate here for the handouts doled out each day by hundreds of tourists. Please do not feed or touch these appealing beggars. It is harmful to the health of the marmots and can be dangerous for you (see the Introduction). After the lodge, the trail forks; stay right and cross the Firehole River. Just after crossing the river, the trail forks again. Take the unpaved trail to the right that ascends a forested slope.

The trail switchbacks up the slope, bringing you quickly to an impressive viewing perch complete with safety rail and tree-stump seats. After you've taken in the view, and hopefully an eruption, continue north 0.3 mile to view Solitary Geyser before you head back to Old Faithful. From Solitary Geyser the trail heads south to Geyser Hill, where an assortment of pools and geysers await. At the junction with the paved trail, turn left. Pass beautiful blue Doublet Pool, and then Giantess Geyser. If you're really lucky, you'll witness one of its dramatic, but infrequent, eruptions. Giantess erupts only two to six times a year, with pre-eruption ground shaking and plumes of water shooting 100 to 200 feet. When Giantess is active, eruptions occur once or twice each hour. After Giantess, continue to the bridge over the Firehole River, and then head back to Old Faithful.

If you want to continue exploring the fascinating Upper Geyser Basin, do *not* recross the Firehole River. Instead, turn right on the paved trail or boardwalk just before the bridge and head northwest to see Beehive Geyser, the Lion Group, and 0.3 mile farther, Grand Geyser. To return to the parking lot from Grand Geyser, just retrace your steps about 200 feet to the trail junction. Then head west across the Firehole River and turn left at the next junction. Pass Castle Geyser and return to Old Faithful via the paved path. This worthwhile tour adds 0.9 mile to your hike.

For additional hiking suggestions in the Upper Geyser Basin, consult the *Upper Geyser Basin Guide*. Remember, while at the basin, watch your children carefully and *never* leave the boardwalk or paved trail. In addition, do not throw any object, even a coin, into any thermal feature. Even small objects can cause severe and irreparable damage.

:27:

Upper Geyser Basin

DIFFICULTY: easy

🚲 DISTANCE: 1.5 miles one way to Morning Glory Pool,
1.9 miles one way additional to Biscuit Basin
USAGE: high
STARTING ELEVATION: 7,340 feet; no elevation gain
SEASON: late May to early October
MAP: USGS 7.5-minute Old Faithful, WY

This effortless bike ride tours the fascinating Upper Geyser Basin. Because of the crowds, this ride is best done in the early morning. The level terrain and good surfaces make this an excellent trip for young children. Before you depart, check at the visitor center for predicted eruption times, particularly of Castle, Riverside, and Daisy geysers, and pick up an Upper Geyser Basin Guide, available from dispensers outside the center. Start at the Old Faithful Visitor Center as described in Trip 26.

Begin your ride by heading northwest (left) along the paved walkway. Pass the Old Faithful Inn on your left and ride toward Castle Geyser, about 0.7 mile. Castle Geyser was named for the cone's resemblance to a ruined castle. It is an especially fine geyser to watch, having a long and powerful eruption. Across the boardwalk from the bike path is Grand Geyser and several smaller thermal features. To visit this group, you must leave your bike; riding is prohibited on the boardwalks.

Next ride north along the Firehole River to the intersection with the boardwalk to the Giant–Grotto Group. Ride past Grotto Geyser and cross the bridge over the river to visit Morning Glory Pool. On the way you'll pass Riverside Geyser, whose frequent eruptions arch impressively over the Firehole River.

Backtrack on the bike path to see Grotto Geyser. If you want to extend your ride, turn right on the paved path just after Grotto Geyser that leads to the Daisy Geyser Group. (Those who want to return should continue riding south on the path back to the visitor center.) Before you reach Daisy Geyser, turn right on the dirt path that runs north alongside the Firehole River. Take this gentle path for 1.9 miles until its intersection with the Grand Loop Road. At this

Lone Star Geyser

junction, you may either proceed on foot to Biscuit Basin (no bikes allowed) or ride back via the bike path to the visitor center.

28

Lone Star Geyser

DIFFICULTY: moderate
DISTANCE: 2.3 miles one way
USAGE: moderate
STARTING ELEVATION: 7,580 feet; elevation gain
160 feet
SEASON: late May through early October
MAP: USGS 7.5-minute Old Faithful, WY

Hike or bike a lovely old road along the Firehole River to the active and impressive Lone Star Geyser. Check at the Old Faithful Visitor Center for the geyser's last recorded eruption and its current eruption interval (historically about 3 hours). Good planning brings rich rewards at the end of this delightful trail. Try to visit in the afternoon when a rainbow may be visible in the geyser's

To Old
Faithful

Kepler
Cascades

T
P

Old Faithful–West Thumb Road

To West
Thumb

0 · N · .5

MILES

Firehole River

No
bicycles
beyond
this point

Meadow

Hot springs

Lone Star
Geyser

spray. For backpackers, a fine campsite is located just 0.4 mile past the geyser.

Drive 2.7 miles southeast on the Old Faithful–West Thumb Road from the Old Faithful Overpass to reach the turnoff for the

Lone Star Geyser Trailhead. The small parking area is located adjacent to Kepler Cascades. From West Thumb, drive about 14.3 miles northwest on the Old Faithful–West Thumb Road. Find the trail (an old road) at the south end of the parking area.

The road courses through forest untouched by the 1988 fires. Mostly level and with some paving still intact, the road provides an excellent surface for young hikers and mountain bikers. Along both sides of the narrow road, lodgepole pines stand straight and tall. Lewis and Clark named the pine for its use as the supporting element in tepees. Each spring, Native American women cut down young lodgepole, stripped their bark, and allowed them to dry. By fall, the 2- to 3-inch-diameter poles weighed only 7 pounds, but retained their strength. To construct a tepee, fifteen poles were bound at one end, spread at the base, and then covered with buffalo hides. Lodgepole pine is easily recognized by its needles, in bundles of two, and by its tall, straight trunk (it is said to resemble a Christmas tree atop a telephone pole).

The road soon crosses the Firehole River. Flowers grace the riverbank, including purple harebells and red-orange Indian paintbrush. At the intersection with the Spring Creek Trail, stay (right) on the road. At 1.9 miles from the trailhead, the road meets a service road; stay left. One-tenth of a mile farther, pass a pretty meadow on the left. Watch for grazing elk in the meadow, especially early or late in the day. Just 0.5 mile after the junction with the service road, arrive at Lone Star Geyser.

Lone Star's impressive 12-foot-high calcite cone was formed by the continuous deposition of sinter. The process began when hot water dissolved rock (silica) deep beneath the earth. When the hot water rose to the surface, it carried dissolved minerals which precipitated out as the water cooled, leaving a coating on the cone. Lone Star Geyser splashes much of the time, so its cone continues to grow with each dousing of mineral-laden water.

To determine when the geyser will erupt, observe what is happening at the cone. (But do not approach it!) Beginning approximately 1 hour before an eruption, Lone Star spurts water from its cone. After an eruption, the geyser boisterously releases steam. During an eruption, water and steam shoot 25 to 40 feet into the air for about 15 to 20 minutes. (To estimate the time of the next eruption, you can also check the log book for the most recent entry, and then assume eruptions at 3-hour intervals.)

Geyser viewing in the unspoiled backcountry is a whole

different experience than in the developed basins. The event is both wonderful and bizarre, especially at Lone Star Geyser. When viewed from the north, the cone resembles the head of a lion. Shrouded in steam during an eruption, the image is awesome and unforgettable.

Even without an eruption, Lone Star Geyser's location by the scenic Firehole River provides a fine destination and superb picnic spot. Cyclists must turn around here, for bicycles are not allowed in the backcountry beyond this point. Backcountry campers can continue to their campsite; they'll be hearing the eruptions throughout the night.

To return to the trailhead (record your eruption first!), just retrace your steps. Back at the trailhead, be sure to take a short walk north to impressive Kepler Cascades, where the Firehole River tumbles 125 feet down a series of rocky tiers through a narrow canyon. Finally, if you're returning to Old Faithful, drop by the visitor center to tell the ranger the time of the eruption you witnessed.

To reach Lone Star's backcountry campsite, continue south past the geyser, and then follow the trail west for 0.2 mile. The trail turns briefly north and reaches a trail junction in 0.1 mile. Bear left and walk southwest just 0.1 mile to the campsite.

29

Shoshone Lake

DIFFICULTY: moderate
DISTANCE: 3 miles one way
USAGE: moderate
STARTING ELEVATION: 7,920 feet; elevation loss, 120 feet
SEASON: mid-June through September
MAP: USGS 7.5-minute Craig Pass, WY

A pleasant, nearly level hike through meadows and lodgepole forest brings you to the shore of beautiful Shoshone Lake, the second-largest lake in the park. Hike early or late in the day, especially in spring and fall, and you have a good chance of seeing moose in the open meadows north of the lake. There are good campsites for backpackers at the lake.

To reach the Delacy Creek Trailhead, drive 8 miles east of Old Faithful or 9 miles west of West Thumb on the Madison–West Thumb Road. Park in the pullout on the north side of the road. The trail begins on the road's south side.

From the roadside, the trail descends through forest into grassy meadows and follows slow-flowing Delacy Creek. A wide variety of flowers—lavender lupine, creamy yarrow, red-orange Indian paintbrush, and purple aster—adorns the trail. Look also for purple monkshood, a tall flower whose petals resemble the robes and hood of a monk. Monkshood blooms throughout the summer in wet meadows and along streambanks.

Follow the rolling trail as it crosses and recrosses the lazy Delacy. Come upon an open meadow giving you a glimpse of Shoshone Lake in the distance. In the meadows, watch carefully for moose and coyote. Bull moose can reach 7 feet at the shoulder,

"Doghair" lodgepole pine forest

To West
Thumb

Madison - West Thumb Road

P
T

Isa Lake

Delacy Creek

To Old
Faithful

Craig
Pass

0   N   1

MILES

Marsh

Delacy Creek Trail

To
Shoshone
Geyser
Basin

Shoshone
Lake

and their antlers can spread over 4 feet. Each year a bull sprouts this headgear at the rate of up to an inch a day. Bulls shed their antlers each fall, and, as soon as they hit the ground, small mammals greedily consume them for the calcium. The whole rack may disappear overnight.

Despite a moose's somewhat comic appearance, they can be dangerous. Bulls have been known to "tree" hikers during their rut, and cows will aggressively defend their young. It is said that before a cow charges, she sticks out her tongue. Never approach close enough to find out!

Along the trail, look for droppings that resemble chocolate Easter eggs. These are moose droppings. Throughout the winter, moose feed on the tender ends of branches. Their woody diet (the Indian word for moose means "twig eater") produces scat that is remarkably like compressed sawdust. Native Americans and early settlers used moose scat for fuel. It is known for its pleasant piney aroma.

Watch also for waterfowl along Delacy Creek. Look in particular for the regal sandhill crane. This impressive bird stands almost 4 feet tall and has a wing span of 6 to 7 feet. Adults are brown, with long legs and necks, white markings on the face, and an unmistakable red cap. Cranes like to hunt for insects, seeds, roots, and small rodents in the wet meadows along the creek. If you're incredibly lucky, you might happen upon the courtship dance of two smitten cranes. The huge birds use their long, spindly legs to leap 6 to 15 feet into the air. The dramatic leap is followed by several graceful bows to their partners. Unfortunately, the sandhill crane population has been declining dramatically in the last 50 years as nesting sites are lost to development.

As you approach the lake, the trail once again enters the lodgepole forest. Note the shiny black gravel on the trail. These are pieces of obsidian, a volcanic glass formed when lava flows ran into glacial ice about 75,000 years ago. Obsidian was very valuable to Native Americans, who fashioned it into razor-sharp arrowheads. Obsidian arrowheads from Yellowstone have been found as far away as the Ohio River valley. Today, obsidian is crafted into high-tech blades used in the most delicate surgery. Far north of this trail, on the Norris–Mammoth Road, you can visit Obsidian Cliff, where a large deposit of obsidian remains to this day.

Finally, the trail leaves the forest to arrive at Shoshone Lake.

The lake was named for the tribe of Native Americans originally residing southwest of Yellowstone. Shoshone Lake is said to be the largest lake in the country with no roads leading to it. The large lake hosts a healthy population of water birds and brown, brook, and lake trout. On its western shore is an impressive geyser basin with a few active geysers. The geyser basin is about 6 miles away via the lake's north shore trail. Easier exploring is immediately accessible by strolling the beach in any direction. To return to the trailhead, simply retrace your steps.

Riddle Lake

DIFFICULTY: moderate
DISTANCE: 2.5 miles one way
USAGE: low
STARTING ELEVATION: 7,988 feet; no elevation gain
SEASON: mid-June through September
MAP: USGS 7.5-minute Mount Sheridan, WY

The trail to Riddle Lake is pleasant and tranquil. Meadows near the lake provide good opportunities to see moose and waterfowl. Since the trail traverses grizzly habitat, check with a ranger at the Grant Visitor Center for closures or restrictions prior to hiking, especially in spring and early summer. This trail is best hiked in late summer when the meadows have dried and biting insects decrease. Here is a riddle for Riddle Lake: Who was richer, the famous naturalist John Muir or railroad magnate Averell Harriman? The answer is found below.

The Riddle Lake Trailhead is located about 3 miles south of the Grant Village intersection on the east side of the West Thumb–South Entrance Road.

The trail begins at the northeast end of the parking area. Follow the trail northeast through fire-touched woods. Forest regrowth is striking in vibrant greens and pink. Watch for elk enjoying the bright fireweed. Almost immediately the trail crosses the Continental Divide. You are unlikely to notice, however, since there is nearly no elevation change. Snaking across Yellowstone, but lacking a precipitous crest, the Continental Divide passes through the park with little drama. Its significance, nevertheless, is profound. All water to the east (or north) of the divide eventually flows to the Atlantic Ocean via the Missouri and Mississippi rivers. All water to the west (or south) of the divide flows into the Snake and Columbia rivers and eventually to the Pacific Ocean.

The question of water flow is the real riddle behind the name of the lake. Early explorers believed that this lake drained to both sides of the Continental Divide, until the discovery of its outlet stream, Solution Creek. Riddle Lake, in fact, drains to the Atlantic.

Proceed through the forest amid seasonal wildflowers, including yarrow, asters, and lupine. Watch for wildlife as you pass small meadows. Arrive at a large marshy area just before reaching the lake. Then follow the trail east to reach the north shore of Riddle Lake. Pond lilies cover much of the lake's surface. This is prime moose habitat. The north side of the lake is also a prime picnic spot as the view to the south encompasses Mount Sheridan and the Red Mountains. Watch also for waterfowl, including white pelicans, goldeneye ducks, and Canada geese.

The severe burn visible on the southeast side of the lake was a hot spot of the Snake River Complex fire that burned much of the forest from West Thumb to the South Entrance. In July of 1988, the Snake River Complex forced the evacuation of tourists

Girl launching a homemade boat

from Grant Village. Although a few buildings were touched, Grant Village was largely spared. Today the Grant Visitor Center has an excellent exhibit describing the fires of 1988.

While picnicking by the lake, you may recognize a particularly familiar and pleasant scent. It comes from the field mint that grows profusely along the lakeshore. Plants in the mint family can be easily recognized by their square stems, opposite leaves, and irregular flowers. Aromatic oils of the mint have long been used as medicines and as food and beverage flavorings by Native Americans and Europeans.

To return to the trailhead, simply retrace your steps. Before you head back, you've earned the answer to the riddle: The wise conservationist John Muir once said about Averell Harriman, "I'm richer than he is. I have all the money I want, and he doesn't."

CHAPTER

5

North Grand Teton

The northern portion of Grand Teton National Park offers spectacular mountain scenery, dominated by majestic Mount Moran. Beautiful Jackson Lake and the scenic Snake River provide plentiful water recreation. The area boasts several gentle hiking trails, excellent backcountry sites for camping, and two easy canoe/kayaking trips.

This relatively small area sees quite a bit of visitation from those staying at nearby campgrounds (Lizard Creek, Colter Bay, Signal Mountain), lodges (Jackson Lake, Signal Mountain), and cabins (Colter Bay, Jackson Lake). Boating and horseback riding are immensely popular. The NPS also offers numerous worthwhile programs. Take advantage of the many lectures, campfire programs, and guided hikes and boat trips offered by rangers at Colter Bay and Signal Mountain.

Set off on your own to find terrifically scenic lakes and wildlife (including trumpeter swans) by hiking in the Colter Bay area (Trips 32 and 33). A superb lakeside campsite can be found just off the latter trail. Canoeists can try the often gentle waters of sheltered Colter Bay (Trip 34) or float a fairly quiet section of the Snake River (Trip 35). There are also two very short walks that offer good views and possible moose (Trip 36) or scenic river habitat and possibly beaver (Trip 37). Finally, hikers and backpackers can drive out to Togwotee Pass to find a hike and campsite in a strikingly different setting with the possibility of a little more solitude (Trip 31).

Lastly, for a magnificent view at sunset, drive to the top of Signal Mountain, just south of the Jackson Lake Dam. The 7,593-foot summit gives you expansive views of Jackson Hole and the surrounding ranges.

Jade Lakes

DIFFICULTY: easy
DISTANCE: 2 miles one way to Upper Jade Lake; 2.5 miles one way to Lower Jade Lake
USAGE: low
STARTING ELEVATION: 9,100 feet; elevation gain, 432 feet
SEASON: mid-June through September
MAP: USGS 7.5-minute Togwotee Pass, WY

Set high in the Absarokas, the lovely Jade Lakes lie under dramatically eroded breccia cliffs. Although nearly an hour's drive from Moran Junction, this trail's dramatic setting and relative isolation is well worth the effort. Visit in August when glorious wildflowers are at their peak. For backpacking families, this short trail leads to superb lakeshore campsites at Upper Jade Lake, only 2 miles from the trailhead.

From Moran Junction, drive east toward Dubois on U.S. 26–287 for about 32 miles to Brooks Lake Road, an unpaved road on the left leading to Brooks Lake Recreation Area (Road 515), 7.8 miles east of Togwotee Pass. Follow Brooks Lake Road about 5.2 miles to Brooks Lake Campground, but do not enter the campground. Turn left (northwest) toward the campground, but stay west to reach a parking area at the south end of Brooks Lake, where you'll find the trailhead.

Head northwest on the wide trail running alongside Brooks Lake, marked for Brooks Lake/Cub Pass. To the east, stratified cliffs rise thousands of feet above the lake. Thirty-eight million to fifty million years ago, Absaroka volcanoes poured layers of volcanic ash and lava over the range. This mixture of rock, ash, and mud hardened into a rock called breccia. Wind, water, and ice sculpted the breccia into shear cliffs and dramatic pinnacles. Its volcanic layers are visible today in handsome bands of purple, red, and brown.

The Absaroka Range (pronounced Ab-sar-O-ka) was named for the Crow Indians. In their native language, Absaroka meant "people of the great winged bird." The Crow inhabited lands to the north along the Yellowstone River. Originally farmers in North Dakota, the Crow migrated to the plains when they acquired horses in the mid-1700s. Known as superb horsemen, the Crow adapted rapidly to a nomadic plains culture that revolved around bison hunting.

After just 0.5 mile, the trail forks. Stay to the left (northwest) for Jade Lakes and follow several parallel paths up a steep, open hillside for 0.5 mile. At the top of the rise, the trail forks again. Take the left fork along the forested ridge. The trail levels off and provides good views of Brooks Lake and its magnificent cliffs.

The trail travels west briefly through lodgepole forest and then swings northwest by a meadow that blooms profusely in mid to late summer. Reenter a mixed forest of pine and fir, and then approach a small pond on the right. Stop a moment to check for tracks in the mud at the pond's edge. You are likely to see the 3-inch heart-shaped prints of mule deer. Closer inspection of the murky pond might reveal tiger salamanders and spotted, boreal, and chorus frogs.

Travel through another meadow bursting with bright flowers, and then arrive at Upper Jade Lake. Once again the magnificent banded cliffs rise spectacularly thousands of feet above the water. Come early in the morning to see a perfect reflection on the still, green lake. The trail along the east side of the lake allows for easy exploring.

To find excellent campsites, continue north on the trail along the lakeshore. (Fine sites are also found on its southwestern shore.) To continue on to Lower Jade Lake, follow the trail another 0.5 mile northeast. Cross the outlet creek at Upper Jade Lake's northern end, and then descend somewhat steeply to the east. Although Lower Jade Lake lacks the dramatic cliffs of Upper Jade, it receives fewer visitors and offers additional fishing opportunities. To return to the trailhead, retrace your steps.

As you drive back to Moran Junction, observe herds of cattle grazing in the Teton National Forest. Livestock grazing on public land takes its toll on the ecosystem. Native wildlife must compete with cattle for limited forage. Ranchers must divert rivers and streams to irrigate fields to produce hay to feed livestock. This diversion of water hurts local fish populations. Furthermore, cattle trample streambanks and hasten erosion near water sources. This leads to sedimentation of streams, which further damages fish habitat. Finally, the protection of grazing livestock leads to the need for predator control. This endangers native species such as bears, coyotes, mountain lions, eagles, and wolves. All activities permitted in the national forests of the GYE, including ranching, mining, logging, and recreation, should be evaluated for their potential negative impacts on the greater ecosystem.

32

Swan Lake and Heron Pond Loop

DIFFICULTY: easy
DISTANCE: 3-mile loop
USAGE: high
STARTING ELEVATION: 6,780 feet; elevation gain,
  80 feet
SEASON: late May through early October
MAP: USGS 7.5-minute Colter Bay, WY

The walk to Swan Lake and Heron Pond is one of the finest family hikes in Grand Teton National Park. The terrain is gentle and the scenery glorious. Go in early morning or evening for the best chance of seeing moose and trumpeter swans. Also highly

Hikers near Heron Pond

recommended are the ranger-led hikes to Swan Lake conducted daily from the Colter Bay Visitor Center. For a longer hike, combine this outing with the trail to Hermitage Point, described in Trip 33.

From Jackson Lake Junction, drive north 5.5 miles on U.S. 89–191–287 to Colter Bay Village. Turn left and follow the Colter Village Road to the parking lot at its western end. Drive to the south end of the parking lot, near the marina. At the lot's south end, look for the Hermitage Point Trailhead sign at the start of an old service road.

Begin walking southwest on the service road where beautiful views of Colter Bay are framed by lodgepole pine. At 26,000 acres, Jackson Lake is the largest lake in Grand Teton. In its natural state, the glacier-carved lake was only 17,000 acres, but in 1905 a dam was built at its outlet, financed by drought-prone Idaho farmers. The dam raised the level of the lake 39 feet, and today Idaho agri-business controls the water level. Consequently, in late summer when farmers need water, the lake falls considerably, forcing closure of marinas and wreaking havoc on tiny amphibians.

Across the lake, Mount Moran (12,605 feet), the fourth-tallest peak in the Teton Range, dominates the horizon. On its face hangs Skillet Glacier, named for its frying-pan shape. Mount Moran has a distinctive flat top and a black stripe of volcanic rock that runs clear to Idaho. The mountain was named for Thomas Moran, a landscape painter and member of the 1870 Yellowstone Expedition. Moran's monumental paintings helped convince Congress to establish Yellowstone as the world's first national park.

At 0.4 mile, arrive at a junction and bear right. In this vicinity look for subalpine fir, an evergreen whose needles are short and flat and whose cones stand erect. In winter, moose and deer browse all reachable needles and twigs of the fir. Since deep snow covers the lowest branches, the animals browse only the center of the tree. The moose and deer thus create a "skirted" shape, seen commonly on firs throughout the park.

Less than 0.1 mile farther, come to a second trail junction and again keep right. Immediately following is a third junction. The left fork leads directly to Heron Pond on a level trail. The right fork also leads to Heron Pond but on the way rises 80 feet to a lookout over Jackson Lake. The view of the Tetons is beautiful from the rise.

Take either trail for 0.4 mile until they join again near the

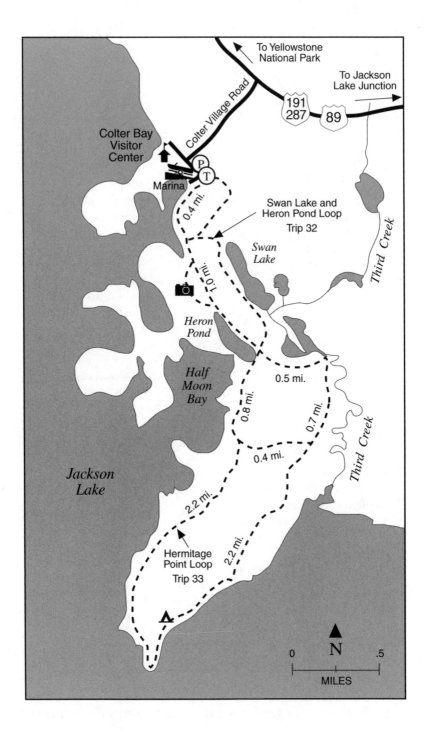

To Yellowstone
National Park

To Jackson
Lake Junction

191
287   89

Colter Village Road

Colter Bay
Visitor
Center

Marina

P
T

0.4 mi.

Swan Lake and
Heron Pond Loop
Trip 32

Swan
Lake

1.0 mi.

Third Creek

Heron
Pond

Half
Moon
Bay

0.5 mi.

0.8 mi.

0.7 mi.

0.4 mi.

Third Creek

Jackson
Lake

2.2 mi.

2.2 mi.

Hermitage
Point Loop
Trip 33

N

0   .5

MILES

north end of Heron Pond. (Those on the overlook trail should bear right at the junction.) Travel briefly through a dense forest of lodgepole pine. Look on trunks for large bare patches, a sign that porcupine have eaten the pine's inner bark. Although porcupines waddle awkwardly on the ground, they climb trees with surprising speed and agility, using long curved claws and their stout tails like a fifth foot. Even so, wildlife biologists claim that, not infrequently, porcupines fall out of trees. Heads up!

Watch for more evidence of wildlife in the lodgepole forest. Bark removed from trunks of younger pines is a likely sign of deer, elk, or moose. These creatures choose small and flexible trees to rub the velvet off their antlers.

Shortly, arrive at Heron Pond (just 1 mile from the trailhead). The pond is covered with pond lilies, an important source of food for wildlife. Ducks eat its large seeds and muskrats gather its rootstalks. Native Americans also enjoyed eating the thick stalks. Indian women waded into the water to cut the rootstalks, or they raided the caches of muskrats. In Scandinavia, they tell of a troll, Näck, who waits at the bottom of ponds, fishing for people to eat. His bait is the yellow pond lily and his line is the rootstalk. The pond lily in Scandinavia is called the "Näck rose."

Pond lilies are considered successional plants, for after they have grown in a pond for a long time, plant material and silt build up, filling in the pond and hastening its transition to meadow. Over the years, shallow Heron Pond will continue to shrink and silt up, eventually forming a moist, flower-filled meadow.

The trail continues along the flowered east shore of Heron Pond. The view west of the Teton Range is magnificent. Visible are Mount Moran and the peaks of the Grand, Middle, and South Tetons. The Shoshone aptly called this range "Teewinot," meaning "many pinnacles." Look to the far side of Heron Pond to locate the remnants of an old beaver lodge.

At the south end of Heron Pond, arrive at a trail junction. Take the trail to the left (north) that leads to Swan Lake in 0.3 mile. Swan Lake's shallow waters and green vegetation provide prime habitat for moose, who frequently feed there. In the middle of the lake, a beaver lodge sits on a small island. The island also provides nesting grounds for a pair of rare trumpeter swans. The huge, snow-white birds are America's largest waterfowl, having wingspans of up to 7 feet. Once hunted for their glorious plumage, the swans were driven to near extinction early in this century. Because of conservation efforts in Yellowstone and a nearby wildlife refuge, the swans have made a tenuous comeback. To give the swans the greatest chance of producing cygnets, never approach them or their nests. Bring binoculars and consider yourself very fortunate to hear the distinctive "koh-ho, koh-ho, koh-ho" of the trumpeters.

Continue along Swan Lake's west shore, traveling north. In late summer, hikers can sample the sweet whortleberries covering the forest floor. Just north of the lake, meet a three-way trail junction. Take the trail to the right, the shortest route back to the trailhead. Ascend a small hill and pass holding ponds once used for sewage treatment.

Descend to the last trail junction and stay left. From this junction, it is only 0.1 mile to the trailhead. For further exploring in the area and the opportunity for backcountry camping, take the 8.8-mile Hermitage Point Loop (Trip 33).

33

Hermitage Point Loop

DIFFICULTY: strenuous
DISTANCE: 8.8-mile loop
USAGE: low
STARTING ELEVATION: 6,780 feet; elevation gain, 160 feet
SEASON: late May through early October
MAP: USGS 7.5-minute Colter Bay, WY

This lengthy trail takes hikers to the flowered meadows and forests of Hermitage Point where terrific views of the Tetons abound. For backpackers, there is a stunning lakeside campsite 4.7 miles from the trailhead. This is an excellent hike for wildlife: look for mule deer, moose, elk, coyote, sandhill cranes, great blue herons, porcupine, and beaver. Be aware that bears also inhabit the area and take appropriate precautions.

Start at the Hermitage Point Trailhead, as described in Trip 32. Follow Trail 32 to the southeast end of Heron Pond (see map

Campsite at Hermitage Point

on p. 151). At the trail junction for Swan Lake, head south for Hermitage Point.

Enter dense forest and walk south through mixed stands of lodgepole, spruce, and fir. In August, tiny purple grouse whortle-berries sweeten this section of trail. Pass a small meadow with superb views of Mount Moran.

Travel about 2 miles farther until the forest finally gives way to sage-covered meadows and dazzling views of the Teton Range. Sun-kissed hills of flowers climb from the water's edge. Purple larkspur and lupine, vanilla buckwheat, and bright red skyrocket gilia light up the grasses. Relatively few hikers make the long trek to Hermit-age Point, so you'll have this magical place mostly to yourself.

From the point, there's a good view of all the major peaks of the range. From this angle, the closest mountain, Mount Moran (12,605 feet), dominates, although the Grand at 13,770 feet is actually taller. The Grand's Matterhorn-like peak (the second highest in Wyoming) is a magnet for climbers world-wide. The grueling climb is often made immensely difficult by sudden strong and frigid storms, even in summer. In midsummer 1985, three experienced climbers froze to death on the Grand when blinding snow and hurricane-force winds swept the summit.

Next climb a small hill and round the point to head north. The glorious hiking continues across meadows dotted with large Dou-glas firs. At 4.7 miles from the trailhead, pass a campsite with tremendous views of both the Gros Ventre Range to the southeast and the Tetons to the west. Prominent on the eastern horizon is Sleeping Indian, a Gros Ventre peak that resembes the reclining figure of a chief with headdress. This is truly a heavenly place to camp and a fabulous place to watch the sunset.

After hiking about a mile along the lakeshore, the trail bends back into the forest. After another mile, arrive at a fork. Stay right to hike along winding Third Creek. Skirt the edge of the wet meadows, thick with willows by the creek. This is superb moose habitat. You may also see the rare trumpeter swan in the creek's waters and ponds. In the drier areas of meadow look for hunting coyote.

Seven-tenths of a mile from the trail junction, arrive at another fork. This time take the left fork to head toward the south end of Heron Pond. After 0.5 mile, reach the pond and another trail junction. At this junction, take the trail to the right, heading north to Swan Lake. From Swan Lake, follow the directions found in Trip 32 to return to the trailhead.

34

Colter Bay

DIFFICULTY: moderate
DISTANCE: approximately 2 miles one way to Half
  Moon Bay
USAGE: high
STARTING ELEVATION: 6,780 feet
SEASON: late May to late September
MAP: USGS 7.5-minute Colter Bay, WY

For a wonderful day's outing, paddle beneath towering Mount Moran among Jackson Lake's terrifically scenic islands and bays. Bring a fishing rod, picnic, and binoculars for watching bald eagles and the occasional moose. From the Colter Bay marina, it's only a 2-mile paddle to gentle Half Moon Bay. Although the bay is often calm, sudden storms and high winds can develop at any time. For your safety, check water conditions and weather reports before you depart, don't venture too far from shore, and always wear life vests. In addition, the water level of Jackson Lake fluctuates by about 10 feet, being lowest in early fall. Consequently, boaters may have to portage in August and September. Check at the marina for current conditions. And don't forget to bring a map!

Drive to the Colter Bay Marina as described in Trip 32. If you're carrying your own boat, find the launch just left of the marina store.

Canoe rentals are available at the marina. The route described below (4 miles round trip) is easily accomplished by canoe in 2 hours (without stops) with one child and one adult paddling.

From the marina, paddle southwest through the narrow channel. Once beyond the protected waters, continue southwest about

0.5 mile to the end of the land mass to the south. Turn between the mainland and an unnamed island to the west. As you glide through the channel, watch the forests and meadows for elk and deer. In early summer, you may see both with their spotted young. At any point along the trip, feel free to beach your vessel and explore.

After another 0.5 mile, slip through a second narrow channel (you may have to portage here) to enter the northern reaches of Half Moon Bay. In front of you is another small unnamed island. Bird life is plentiful here. You can't miss the abundant California gulls who migrate from the Pacific Coast to summer in the Tetons. Watch also for osprey and the American white pelican. The white pelican is awkward on land, but graceful in flight. Unlike its cousin, the brown pelican, the white does not dive for its dinner. With its oversized yellow bill, it scoops up 2-foot trout, suckers, minnows, and occasionally salamanders while cruising across the water. Pelicans seen in Colter Bay come from a protected nesting colony on the Molly Islands in Yellowstone Lake.

Paddle around the island, and then head back to the marina by the same route you came. For a longer paddle, continue southwest, and then northwest to pass Sheffield Island, returning to the marina via Little Mackinaw Bay. The extra touring will add about 1 mile to your trip.

35

Snake River Float (Jackson Lake Dam to Pacific Creek Landing)

DIFFICULTY: moderate
DISTANCE: 5 to 6 miles one way (trip is one way only)
USAGE: moderate
STARTING ELEVATION: 6,800 feet
SEASON: late May to late September
MAP: USGS 7.5-minute Moran, WY

This serenely beautiful float trip is especially memorable in the early morning when there are good chances of seeing moose, great blue herons, beaver, osprey, and bald eagles. While this trip is fine for novices, all paddlers must be prepared to make a strong and timely exit at Pacific Creek Landing. After Pacific Creek, the Snake River's current increases substantially, generating dangerous conditions for novices. Before departing, obtain a boat permit, secure life vests for all passengers, and inquire about river flow. Allow a few hours for the float.

Drive to Pacific Creek Landing, 3.4 miles southeast of Jackson Lake Junction on U.S. 89–287. Take a good look at the landing and observe how Pacific Creek enters the Snake River to the north. Boaters need to paddle across swift current just after the entry of Pacific Creek to reach the landing safely. Observe landmarks and signage in this area to ensure that you will recognize the landing in time. If you have two cars, leave one in the lot, and drive northwest 4.4 miles to the last turnout before Jackson Lake Dam. The put-in is directly below the dam.

Begin your trip by launching downstream and floating with the current. It is said that the best fishing in the Snake River is in this spot directly below the dam. American white pelicans seem to agree, judging by the crowd usually congregated at the foot of the dam. Anglers and pelicans, as well as eagles and osprey, fish for the Snake's cutthroat, rainbow, and brook trout. Pass under Cattleman's Bridge, originally used for driving cattle across the river. The bridge now provides access to the east side of Signal Mountain.

Just after the bridge, float down to Oxbow Bend on your left for a paddling detour in its calm waters. Look along the willow-choked banks for moose, otter, beaver, and muskrat. Don't be surprised to see a moose partially or wholly submerged in the river. Moose love the soggy aquatic plants growing on the river bottom and will readily dive for them (as deep as 25 feet). Moose are well-adapted for swimming. Their coats are water resistant, keeping them comfortably warm in the cold water, and one layer of their hair is hollow, giving them great buoyancy.

The Oxbow Bend is superb bird habitat. Watch for Canada geese, bald eagles, trumpeter swans, numerous songbirds, and great blue herons. The 4-foot-tall herons have a graceful, smoky blue body, long neck, and endless, sticklike legs. They stalk fish, insects, and frogs along the water's edge. Cruise this area quietly. Herons are particularly vulnerable to human disturbance.

Bald eagles are also very vulnerable. When rangers discover an eagle's nest in Grand Teton National Park, they limit human

activity in the area to allow the eagles to breed. Mature bald eagles of both sexes (4- to 5-years old) have black wings, snow-white head and tail, and bright yellow beak and eyes. Immature bald eagles are brown and are often mistaken for golden eagles and osprey. Look for bald eagles in tall trees above the river. After exploring

Getting ready to float the Snake River

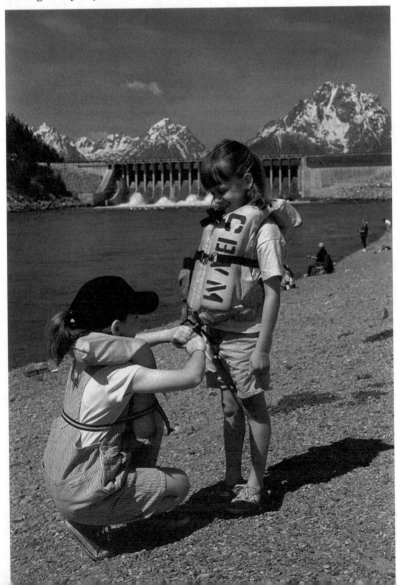

the Oxbow Bend, paddle back out into the current to continue your float. Pass Buffalo Meadows, where moose and abundant bird life can also be seen. The confluence of Pacific Creek is about 1.75 miles downstream of Oxbow Bend. Paddlers should watch for the creek well in advance.

The safest way to reach Pacific Creek Landing is to stay close to the Snake River's left bank. After the entrance of Pacific Creek, paddle hard to cross its current and exit the river on the left bank, at the landing just downstream.

For a truly magical trip, experienced boaters should make this trip under a full moon.

Willow Flats Overlook

DIFFICULTY: very easy
DISTANCE: 0.5 mile one way
USAGE: high
STARTING ELEVATION: 6,840 feet; elevation gain,
    80 feet
SEASON: late May through early October
MAP: USGS 7.5-minute Two Ocean Lake, WY

This very easy hike ascends tiny Lunchtree Hill for views of Willow Flats, the Tetons, and Jackson Lake. Lunchtree Hill is a convenient picnic spot for those staying at or near Jackson Lake Lodge. Come at dusk or dawn for striking views of sunlit mountains, and bring your binoculars to search the flats for moose. The hike is not recommended for midday in summer, for the shadeless trail can grow quite hot. Try it in fall for views of brilliant red-gold foliage.

Drive to Jackson Lake Lodge, located just off U.S. 89–191–297, 1 mile north of Jackson Lake Junction. Enter the lodge, walk through the lobby, and exit the building on its west side. Find the paved trail to the right of the building.

Begin on the paved trail and climb to the top of Lunchtree Hill through the sagebrush community. Crush a few leaves of this pervasive shrub and smell the pungent aroma to see how it got its name. Sagebrush is critical winter food for pronghorn antelope, and it provides food and shelter for a variety of smaller creatures as well, such as the snowshoe hare, least chipmunk, Unita ground squirrel, and sage grouse. Colorful flowers grow among the sagebrush, including red-orange Indian paintbrush, yellow arrowleaf balsamroot, and blue harebell.

Once on top of the hill, visit the monument commemorating the historic meeting in 1926 of John D. Rockefeller and family and Horace Albright, superintendent of Yellowstone National Park. At this site, above beautiful Jackson Lake and under towering Mount Moran, the group discussed the inclusion of the Tetons into the national park system. The dream was finally realized 26 years later, after years of controversy and through generous land donations from the Rockefeller family.

Scan the willow-filled wetland to the west for moose. Moose love the soggy area, filled with tasty willow for them to eat. In summer, they frequently stand knee-deep in mud, lazily pulling up soggy green plants (dubbed "moose muck") and munching them contentedly. Visitors, in fact, rarely see a moose's full body, for its legs are either underwater or obscured by thick underbrush. Their thin, gangly legs are specially jointed to allow them to walk easily in deep snow or mud. A moose can lift its leg out of the same hole in which it was placed, so that it doesn't waste energy unnecessarily.

To hike north of Lunchtree Hill, follow informal trails through the sagebrush. Explore the level bluff, heading north until the trail becomes indistinct and begins to descend into trees. At that point, about 0.5 mile from Jackson Lake Lodge, turn around and return to the lodge.

Schwabacher's Landing

DIFFICULTY: very easy
DISTANCE: 0.5 mile one way
USAGE: moderate
STARTING ELEVATION: 6,420 feet; elevation gain, 20 feet
SEASON: late May through mid-October
MAP: USGS 7.5-minute Moose, WY

Stroll along an incredibly scenic tributary of the Snake River to explore beaver dams, flowers, and waterfowl. Arrive at sunset for the chance to see elk, moose, coyote, and bison under a sky framed by the Teton's most majestic peaks. Bring a fishing rod to try for trout in this angler's paradise. This trail makes a superb and effortless late afternoon outing.

From Moose Junction, drive north 4.5 miles on U.S. 191–89–26 to the turnoff for Schwabacher's Landing on the left. From Moran Junction, drive 13.5 miles south on U.S. 191–89–26 to the turnoff. Turn west onto the dirt road and drive 1.1 miles to a small parking area. The informal trail begins near the river.

Head north (right) on the narrow trail. Above the swift river soars the spectacular Cathedral Group (the trio of Grand Teton, Mount Owen, and Teewinot). Almost immediately, find the first of three beaver dams. Beavers build dams to provide quiet water for food gathering and a safe haven for their lodges. A pair of beavers can build an average-sized dam, 2 feet high by 12 feet long, in just *two* nights.

Beavers are nocturnal; their activity usually begins at dusk. Beavers were originally diurnal (active during the day), but intensive trapping in the early 1800s changed their habits. In those days, men's stovepipe hats, constructed of fine felt from beaver pelts, were the rage. After trappers nearly exterminated the beaver east of the Mississippi, mountain men came to the Rockies seeking the luxurious chestnut fur, nicknamed "soft gold." They might have wiped out the western beaver also, but men's fashion fortunately turned to silk, and North America's largest rodent was saved.

Your best chance of seeing beaver is in the fall. Beavers do not hibernate, so they must stockpile a large reserve of food for the winter. On autumn days, beavers can be seen cutting and dragging aspen branches to their underwater cache beneath their lodge. A family of nine beavers gathers literally a *ton* of bark to carry it through until spring.

Look and listen for signs of beaver. A domed lodge, constructed of sticks and mud, is the most obvious. Look also for conical tree stumps with teeth marks, peeled limbs where beaver chewed off the bark, and scent mounds (hills of mud and sticks about 1 foot high by 3 feet wide) that mark a beaver's territory. Listen for the resounding slap of a beaver's flat, hairless tail on the water. It sounds the family alarm, warning others of your presence.

Follow the narrow trail upstream along the grassy bank. Flat, Frisbee-sized patties—"buffalo chips"—often litter the path. These were left by the small herd of bison that inhabits the park. Native Americans and settlers burned the chips as fuel.

In the early 1800s, 40-to 60-million bison roamed the western plains. Beginning in the mid-1800s, settlers shot the herds wholesale to attain hides and to deprive the Plains Indians of their means of survival. Tribes depended upon bison for their food, shelter, tools, weaponry, warm clothing, and bedding. Indians used nearly every part of the animal. Visitors can view fascinating bison artifacts from this era at Colter Bay's Indian Art Museum.

By 1889 bison were nearly extinct; less than one hundred survived in a remote part of Yellowstone National Park. All bison in the parks today are descendants of those last few. Currently the GYE bison population hovers around two thousand.

Serious threats to bison still exist. Bison carry brucellosis, a disease that causes miscarriage in domestic cattle. Even though there has *never* been a documented case of bison passing the disease to cattle (and experts believe it would be highly unlikely), local ranchers fear the presence of free-ranging bison. Consequently, they are exerting great pressure to reduce the size of Yellowstone's herd.

Continue to walk north along the creek. Arrive at a second, much older beaver dam. Check for waterfowl, most likely mallards, Barrow's goldeneye, and red-breasted mergansers. Be alert also for a small, beaverlike creature, the muskrat. (Watch for its long, thin tail.) The muskrat builds a smaller domed lodge, constructed from cattails, reeds, and mud. Look also for the playful river otter in these environs.

Just 0.25 mile farther, arrive at the third dam. Beyond the dam, the trail fades. This is a good turnaround point. On your return, scan tall trees for the osprey and bald eagles that frequent the Snake River bottomlands. Look down also, in the grass beside the creek, for green garter snakes or the rare rubber boa, both harmless.

CHAPTER

6

South Grand Teton

The southern portion of Grand Teton National Park offers the most breathtaking scenery in the region. Its massive sweep of jagged peaks displays a soaring handsomeness that lifts the spirit. To enter this wilderness is the ultimate adventure. Whether by bike, canoe, or your own two feet, check out the following outings.

There are several short and easy hikes to beautiful lakes (Trips 38, 39, 40, 44) and longer, challenging climbs to steep-walled canyons (Trips 43 and 46). Two bike rides offer spectacular scenery with relatively little effort (Trips 45 and 48). Paddle a canoe or kayak to two beautiful lakes (Trip 38) or take a ferry across one of the park's finest (Trips 41, 42, 43). Lastly, ride an aerial tram to visit the alpine environment (Trip 47).

Other family activities in the park include several self-guided trails. Try Menor's Ferry, where children can be "ferried" across the river in a re-creation of a circa 1890s contraption. Children can also participate in the NPS junior ranger program. Rangers lead children-only adventures weekday afternoons from the visitor centers. In summer, a family picnic and swim at warm and scenic String Lake is the perfect park outing.

There are also family activities offered in and around the nearby town of Jackson. Whitewater rafting on the Snake River is perhaps the most popular. Horseback riding in the park and in the nearby national forests is much in demand. For rainy days, Jackson offers several museums as well as an indoor recreation center and climbing gym.

The region also offers rich evening activites. Early evening is one of the best times to see the numerous deer and elk who inhabit the south park. A quiet moonlight paddle is also highly recommended (Trip 38). For those seeking more structure, the NPS offers numerous evening programs and guided walks. And for a different kind of fun, Jackson hosts biweekly rodeos.

Leigh and Bearpaw Lakes

DIFFICULTY: moderate

DISTANCE: 2.3 miles one way to Leigh Lake Beach, 3.6 miles one way to Bearpaw Lake

USAGE: high

STARTING ELEVATION: 6,870 feet; elevation gain, 30 feet

SEASON: late May through early October

MAP: USGS 7.5-minute Jenny Lake, WY

Leigh Lake is a fabulous family destination. Paddle 3 miles to the north end of Leigh Lake or hike the short, scenic trail for incomparable views of Mount Moran's hanging glaciers and steep-walled canyons. After 2.3 miles, hikers and paddlers are treated to Leigh's postcard-perfect white sand beach where picnics and bathing suits are a must. For backpacking families, there are excellent lakeside campsites. Further exploring in the area brings hikers to pretty Bearpaw Lake. There are only two drawbacks: carry insect repellent and expect company on this gem of a trail.

Begin at the String Lake Picnic Area, located at the north end of the String Lake Parking Area. To find the parking area, drive north 10 miles on the Teton Park Road from the Moose Entrance Station to the turnoff for String Lake, signed "North Jenny Lake

Junction." Turn west at the junction and drive 1.5 miles to the String Lake Parking Area. The parking area is 0.4-mile long, with the picnic area at its north end.

To reach the trailhead, hikers and paddlers must pass the most scenic and warmest swimming hole in Grand Teton, located adjacent to the picnic area. Swimmers should bring a float and wear foot protection, for the bottom is studded with old logs. Boats (oar-powered only) can enter the water at the picnic area or at the canoe launch immediately south of the picnic area.

Find the Leigh Lake Trailhead just north of the picnic area. Head north on the wide trail paralleling the shore. (Paddlers should follow narrow String Lake to its northern end.) Travel 0.9 mile under the shade of lodgepole pine, subalpine fir, and Englemann spruce. In late summer, enjoy tiny grouse whortleberry and sumptuous wild huckleberry growing along the trail. The woods are also sprinkled with delicate, blue harebells (bluebells) that hang gracefully downward and bloom from June through September. Deer, elk, pika, marmot, bear, and snowshoe hare, of course, enjoy eating the harebells.

At the north end of String Lake, arrive at a junction. The left fork heads over Leigh Lake's outlet bridge to Paintbrush Canyon and provides access to Leigh Lake's west shore campsites. Backpackers (sites 13 and 15) should cross the bridge and then turn right onto the unimproved path that follows Leigh Lake's west shore. The campsites are about 1 and 1.5 miles from the bridge, respectively. Campsite 13 is spectacular, having its own sandy beach and grand views of the lake and the Gros Ventre Range.

Hikers take the right fork to Leigh Lake and immediately come upon another junction. Again bear right. (The left fork is for canoe portages.) Enter forest; then climb 20 feet up the sandy slope of Leigh Lake's terminal moraine. The 2-mile long lake is the third largest in the park and one of the deepest at 250 feet. Continue north on a trail paralleling the lakeshore. (There are minor trails in this area; choose the well-defined trail closest to the shore.)

Paddlers should take their vessels out of the water on String Lake's northeast shore, just before the Leigh Lake outlet bridge. At this point, paddlers, carrying their vessels, pick up the Leigh Lake Trail. Take the first left for the short canoe portage to Leigh Lake. Upon re-boarding, paddle along the east shore of Leigh Lake, staying east of the lake's small islands.

Meltwater from Falling Ice Glacier, wedged between the east and west summits of Mount Moran, gives Leigh Lake its greenish hue. The 100-foot thick glacier sends milky glacial "flour" (finely ground rock) to the lake each spring. Falling Ice Glacier is a reminder of the mammoth forces that created Leigh Lake.

Imagine colossal tongues of ice, 1,000 feet tall, pushing down Paintbrush and Leigh canyons, located just south of Mount Moran. At the canyon mouths, the glaciers flowed together, fanned out, and then bulldozed their way east. As the two glaciers melted, the water was held by the moraine, or hill of soil and rock, that the glaciers pushed out in front of them. Hikers follow the moraine as the trail continues north along the lake. Spur trails on the left lead to the lake shore. Continue north 1.3 miles through lush, dense forest to reach the lake's splendid sand beach. Winds blowing continuously (and sometimes ferociously) from Leigh and Paintbrush canyons have battered the rocks on the east shore to fine white sand. On sunny summer days the water is filled with bathers. The lake is also popular with anglers trying for mackinaw and cutthroat trout. In this area, hikers also pass three superb group campsites for parties of seven or more.

Across the lake is majestic Mount Moran, its snow-capped peak rising almost 6,000 feet above the lake. The dark vertical stripe on its face is a 150-foot-wide column of black low-silica rock called "diabase." The diabase formed when molten rock flowed up into a fissure. The diabase extends 77 miles west to the other side of the mountain range. Imagine the heat and force that extruded this tremendous quantity of molten rock.

From Leigh Lake's sand beach, Bearpaw Lake lies 1.5 miles to the north. To reach Bearpaw, continue hiking (or paddling) north. Near the north end of Leigh Lake notice a rocky island with burned snags. In the 1980s, a fire on the island jumped across the water and burned the area north and east of Leigh Lake. Look for osprey atop the tall snags.

At the northernmost tip of Leigh Lake (3.7 miles from the trailhead), hikers arrive at a junction. Paddlers must leave their boats on the north shore to find this intersection. The junction's right fork leads to Bearpaw Lake in approximately 0.3 mile. Follow the trail across a meadow and arrive shortly at the small, quiet lake. The lovely lake is surrounded by pines, its grassy shore delicately flowered in purple and white. Bearpaw is a nice place to explore when Leigh Lake attracts too many visitors.

Energetic hikers may also want to visit tiny Trapper Lake, just 0.8 mile from the trail junction at the north end of Leigh Lake. To reach Trapper, backtrack to the junction and take the left fork. Fine campsites on the north end of Trapper Lake and the northwest side of Bearpaw Lake can be reached from this trail.

—— 39 ——

String Lake to Jenny Lake's West Shore

DIFFICULTY: easy
DISTANCE: 1.7 mile one way
USAGE: moderate
STARTING ELEVATION: 6,880 feet; elevation gain,
    40 feet
SEASON: late May through early October
MAP: USGS 7.5-minute Jenny Lake, WY

    The lush and shady 1.7-mile trail from String Lake to the west shore of Jenny Lake is an excellent alternative to riding the busy

Bridge over String Lake outlet

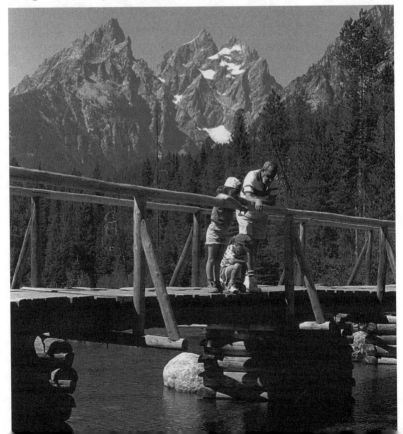

Jenny Lake shuttle boat, especially at peak season. Once at Jenny Lake's west shore, hikers can access trails to Hidden Falls (Trip 41), Inspiration Point (Trip 42), and Cascade Canyon (Trip 43).

To find the String Lake Trailhead, follow the driving directions for Trip 38 to the String Lake Parking Area. Park at the south end where there's a sign for the String Lake Trailhead. Find the trail at the lake's edge and follow it south to the substantial bridge over the String Lake outlet. Views from the bridge of the Cathedral Group (Teewinot, Mount Owen and the Grand) are breathtaking. Continue southwest as the trail cuts through dense thimbleberry bushes, cow parsnip, and purple monkshood. In late summer, when the thimbleberries are ripe, watch for black bears feeding in the brush. In areas of dense vegetation, hikers should make noise to avoid surprising a foraging bear. At 0.3 mile from the trailhead, arrive at a junction. The trail to the right travels along the west shore of String Lake (Trip 40). Take the trail to the left which leads to Jenny Lake.

Head through a lush forest of Engelmann spruce and subalpine fir. Learning to recognize these trees is easy: just "shake hands" with the nearest evergreen, feeling its needles. If the needles are sharp to the touch and squarish, you have met a spruce. If the needles are flat, friendly, and soft (think "fur"), you are holding a fir. If you have encountered a tree with thin, longish needles (2 to 3 inches long) in *bundles* of two, it is a lodgepole pine, for fir and spruce needles are never "bundled." This trail and the trail to Hidden Falls pass some of the oldest and most magnificent Engelmann spruce in the region; some are estimated to be over 400 years old.

Proceed southwest past a variety of moisture-loving flowers, including purple monkshood, coneflower, and giant white cowparsnip. The latter, a member of the parsley family, can grow to 8 feet with umbels of tiny white flowers. Black bears and other large mammals enjoy its leaves and stem. In rocky areas, watch for yellow-bellied marmots. This handsome rodent (a western cousin of the woodchuck) dens in rock piles and is frequently seen on summer days atop the rocks.

Next approach a series of wooden bridges. To the right, an unmarked path by a creek leads to Hanging Canyon, a very difficult 2,800-foot climb from Jenny Lake. Continue southwest over the bridges and, at 1.7 miles from the trailhead, arrive at the junction with the horse trail to Cascade Canyon on the right. Those headed for the canyon (bypassing Hidden Falls and Inspiration Point) should turn right here. The trail into the canyon is described in Trip 43.

For those wishing to visit Hidden Falls and Inspiration Point, continue on the main trail 0.3 mile to the junction with the well-worn trail from the West Shore Boat Dock. Turn right at this junction and follow the trail as described in Trip 41.

It is possible to hike the circumference of Jenny Lake and return to String Lake via Jenny Lake's east shore (a 6.8-mile loop), but it is not recommended. Jenny Lake's east shore trail closely parallels the Jenny Lake Road, so traffic noise is intrusive. The superb trails to Hidden Falls (Trip 41), Cascade Canyon (Trip 43), and the west shore of String Lake (Trip 40) are far more enjoyable.

40

String Lake Loop

DIFFICULTY: easy
DISTANCE: 3.5 miles round trip
USAGE: moderate
STARTING ELEVATION: 6,880 feet; elevation gain, 260 feet
SEASON: late May through early October
MAP: USGS 7.5-minute Jenny Lake, WY

String Lake is a magical spot. Its shallow, swimmable waters and sublime mountain backdrop make it an absolute favorite for all ages. This trail is one of several options for hikers departing from String Lake. Less scenic than Trip 39, this trail is nevertheless enchanting in fall. Those planning to swim in String Lake should bring footwear, for the lake bottom is littered with logs.

Drive to the String Lake Trailhead, as described in Trip 39. Follow Trip 39 to its first trail junction 0.3 mile from the String Lake Trailhead (for trail map, see page 169).

Head right (northwest) at the junction. The trail soon leaves the forest to arrive at the dry and sunny west shore of String Lake. Rise gently and cross a burned slope, now populated by mountain ash and aspen, punctuated by colorful fireweed, aster, arrowleaf balsamroot, and Indian paintbrush. Mount St. John (11,430 feet) rises to the west.

Ascend through sagebrush and aspen as the trail heads north, gaining good views of the Gros Ventre Range to the east and String Lake below. In French, *gros ventre* means "big stomach," and the range was named for the Gros Ventre Indians. The tribe's name was the result of a miscommunication between French trappers and Shoshone Indians. When trappers asked the Shoshone about the tribe living in the neighboring mountain range, the Shoshone motioned to their stomachs to indicate that the tribe was always in a state of hunger. The French assumed that the Shoshone were describing a weight problem, and thus the Gros Ventre tribe was named.

At approximately 1.1 miles from the trailhead, cross a bridge over a stream originating on Rockchuck Peak above you to the west. As you cross the slope of Rockchuck, look below to a marshy area west of String Lake. These wetlands are prime moose habitat. Next, enter again the shade of Douglas fir, mountain ash, and mountain maple, and climb to a junction with the Paintbrush Canyon Trail. At this junction, descend to the right into a dense forest of lodgepole pine.

Red squirrels are plentiful in this pine forest. Look for pine cones stripped of scales lying on the forest floor like discarded corncobs. Enter the squirrels' territory and they assault you with shrill chattering. Their scolding persists until you leave (unless, like a squirrel, you can answer back requesting temporary silence). Every red squirrel, both male and female, defends a territory of 1 to 3 acres, sometimes with physical combat. Only during mating does a female let down her guard and allow a suitor to enter. Look for the squirrels screaming from tree stumps or branches. If you can't locate the source (some seem to have the skill of ventriloquists), listen for the sound of claws scampering up bark.

You may spy the red squirrel's giant middens. A midden is both the squirrel's pantry and his garbage pile, composed of pine, fir, and spruce cones as well as their inedible remains. Buried in the large mound of scales are scores of freshly cut cones, stored for later consumption. Successive generations of squirrels often use the same midden, resulting in piles up to 6 to 10 yards across and 30 inches deep.

Descend gently through the forest for about 0.8 mile to a bridge over the shallow stream connecting String and Leigh lakes. Just before the bridge, find a house-sized boulder to the left of the trail. This is a glacial erratic, a rock carried miles by a descending glacier. The boulder illustrates the power of glaciers to tear, transport, and drop debris from mountaintop to valley. It also provides an irresistible climbing opportunity for youngsters.

Cross the bridge to reach the east shore of String Lake. Then turn right to walk south along the lakeshore. In early morning or at dusk, watch for mule deer. Their large ears give the deer extraordinary hearing. Each ear moves independently to pick up

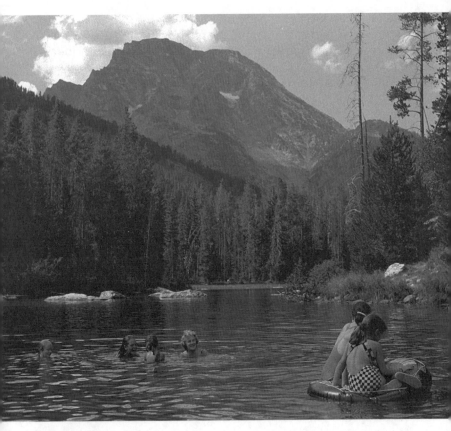

Enjoying String Lake

sounds of potential predators. If a sound is heard, the deer's tail rises to reveal a bright white underside, signaling others of danger. When alarmed, mule deer bound away with lightning speed and amazing grace—all four feet leaving the ground and then landing together—practically flying through dense forest.

From the bridge, it is 0.9 mile to the String Lake Picnic Area. Before leaving the area, let children sample String Lake's warm waters. With magnificent mountains rising from its western shore, this may be the prettiest swimming hole on earth. From the picnic area, follow a patchy trail, interrupted by parking lots and canoe launches, along the lakeshore for 0.3 mile to the start at String Lake Trailhead.

41

Hidden Falls

DIFFICULTY: easy
DISTANCE: 0.5 mile one way via ferry, 2.2 miles one
way from the String Lake Trailhead, 2.5 miles one
way from the East Shore Boat Dock
USAGE: very high
STARTING ELEVATION: 6,794 feet; elevation gain,
160 feet
SEASON: mid-May through early October
MAP: USGS 7.5-minute Jenny Lake, WY

The trail to Hidden Falls is short and sweet. A boat at Jenny
Lake ferries hikers across the lake, saving them 2 miles each way.
Consequently, this trail attracts more hikers than any other in
Grand Teton. To avoid crowds, take the first boat over. For your
effort, you'll be rewarded with solitude and, in late summer, a tasty
treat from the berry bushes lining the lake's west shore. Late ris-
ers should be prepared to wait at the dock as long as 40 minutes
in midsummer. Alternatively, start this hike at the String Lake
Trailhead and travel a scenic 1.7 miles (one way) to the West Shore
Boat Dock (Trip 39). Hikers can also start at the East Shore Boat
Dock and walk around the southwest shore of Jenny Lake, adding 2 miles to the hike each way.

Those starting at Jenny Lake should enter the park via the
Moose Entrance Station and drive north 6.7 miles on the Teton
Park Road to the turnoff for South Jenny Lake. Turn left, drive
toward the ranger station, and park in the large Jenny Lake parking lot. Find the boat dock at the southeast end of Jenny Lake.
Round-trip fares are $4.00 per adult, $2.25 per child, and free for
those under 6. Boats leave every 20 minutes from 8:00 A.M. to 6:00
P.M. For those starting at String Lake, follow the directions for Trip
39 (for trail map, see page 172).

If you're hiking from the East Shore Boat Dock, proceed west
over the bridge on the clearly marked trail around the lake. This
route is less scenic than the trail starting at String Lake, but it
does give you the option of riding the boat on the way home. On
the west side of the lake, watch for black bears and make noise

when passing the dense berry bushes that line the trail.

After the Jenny Lake shuttle boat delivers you to the West Shore Boat Dock, turn immediately left (south). The trail soon swings west and arrives at a three-way junction (those hiking from the East Shore Boat Dock will arrive at this junction). Continue straight (west) for Hidden Falls. The trail to the right (north) leads to the String Lake Trailhead.

To sample berries before viewing the falls, turn left at the three-way junction and cross Cascade Creek. Continue south along the shore of Jenny Lake keeping left at the next trail junction. In late summer, you can't miss the breast-high bushes of sweet wild raspberries and bright red thimbleberries. When lifted from the plant, thimbleberries fit on the thumb just like a thimble! The park allows picking for personal consumption; just be considerate of the many hungry hikers and creatures following you. Watch for bears.

After berry picking, return to the first junction and then travel west, crossing Cascade Creek on a substantial bridge. At the bridge, watch for water ouzels, or American dippers. This chunky brown bird, which resembles a tailless robin, likes to dive in rushing water in search of small fish and insects. The superbly adapted dipper is able to walk on the bottom of streams, swim underwater, and fly behind waterfalls. After a dip, the ouzel hops on a rock and bobs up and down. Ouzels build their nests on rocky ledges, often within the spray of a waterfall, where their eggs are safe from predators. Look for the entertaining ouzel throughout the park, whenever you encounter a small, swift stream. Listen for its cheerful "zreet!"

Meet another trail junction and continue straight (west). Follow the trail as it curves north and look for a spur trail on the left, signed for Hidden Falls (located just before another bridge). The spur trail leads hikers 50 feet to the falls. Flanking the path are tall purple monkshood, a colorful flower whose petals resemble the robes of a monk. Watch on talus slopes to the left for yellow-bellied marmots and tiny pikas.

The pika (6 to 9 inches in length) is a round-eared relative of the rabbit. Except for its large, shiny black eyes, its appearance is distinctly unrabbitlike. Its tiny tail is lost in fur, and it most resembles a small guinea pig. This grayish ball of fur is most often spotted scampering acrobatically over talus slopes. Its rapid rock-hopping owes a debt to the "non-skid" coating of fur on the bottom of its tiny feet.

Hidden Falls does not come into view until you are standing

right before it. The terrific 200-foot cascade is a wonderful surprise. Its rushing rivulets swell with snowmelt in spring and early
summer. If it's not too crowded, the falls is an excellent picnic spot.
For additional entertainment, look north to the rock face where
climbing clinics are regularly held. For those with energy remain-
ing, visit Inspiration Point, a 0.4-mile climb of about 250 feet from
Hidden Falls. At Inspiration Point (Trip 42), hikers have lovely
views east over Jenny Lake and Jackson Hole.

42

Inspiration Point

DIFFICULTY: moderate
DISTANCE: 0.9 mile one way from the West Shore
    Boat Dock, 2.6 miles one way from String Lake
    Trailhead, 2.9 miles one way from the East Shore
    Boat Dock
USAGE: very high
STARTING ELEVATION: 6,794 feet; elevation gain,
    406 feet
SEASON: mid-May through early October
MAP: USGS 7.5-minute Jenny Lake, WY

After visiting Hidden Falls, climb to Inspiration Point for a rewarding view of Jenny Lake and the mountains that surround Jackson Hole. From Inspiration Point, strong hikers can continue to
Cascade Canyon for more terrific scenery and wildlife (Trip 43).

Follow the directions for Trip 41 to Hidden Falls. From the
falls, return to the main trail and cross the bridge over Cascade
Creek. Climb the steep switchbacks that hug the rock face. Proceed with care and watch children closely. In the 1930s, the Ci-
vilian Conservation Corps carved this trail from the granite as part
of a huge trail-building project that contributed hundreds of miles
of trails to the park.

As you ascend, pass lookouts with boulders irresistible to
climbing children. To the west rises the striking trio of mountains
called the Cathedral Group. From left to right are Mount Teewinot

(12,325 feet), Grand Teton (13,770 feet), and Mount Owen (12,928 feet). Five-hundred feet above the valley floor, Inspiration Point affords great views of Jackson Hole. "Hole" is a fur trapper's term meaning "high valley." From this vantage point, one can see the ranges that surround the mostly flat "hole." To the northeast lie the Washakie and Absaroka ranges, to the east sit the Mount Leidy Highlands, and to the southeast lie Sheep Mountain and the Gros Ventre Range.

From Inspiration Point, the whole of Jenny Lake is visible. Jenny Lake is the second-largest lake in the park, smaller only than Jackson Lake. Like Jackson Lake, Jenny Lake was created by a glacier flowing out of a canyon. About 12,000 to 15,000 years ago, consistently cool temperatures produced huge expanses of ice, or glaciers, on the Teton peaks. Gravity eventually drew the glaciers down the mountain. Taking routes of least resistance, the ice slid down river valleys, turning V-shaped valleys into flat-bottomed, U-shaped canyons. Glaciers pushed soil, boulders, and rock down the mountain like a child plowing sand with his hands. At the bottom,

Crossing Cascade Creek

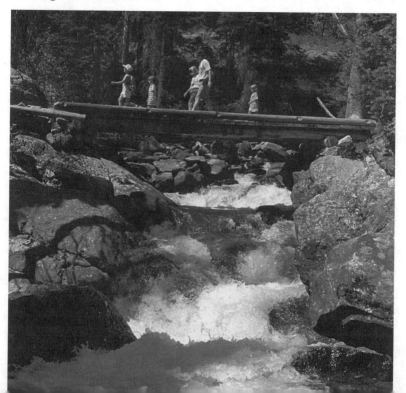

the glacier rested. All around the tongue of ice stood masses of debris, called moraines.

In time, temperatures warmed, the glaciers melted, and the moraines held the water of the melting glacier. Today the moraine still holds the lake's water, which is replenished each spring by fresh snowmelt. Glacier-born lakes lie at the mouths of nearly all the canyons in the Tetons; including Jenny Lake at Cascade Canyon, Leigh Lake at Leigh and Paintbrush canyons, and Bradley Lake at Garnet Canyon.

From Inspiration Point, the trail turns west and enters Cascade Canyon, one of the prettiest trails in the park (Trip 43). Those returning should retrace their steps to the boat dock.

Forks of Cascade Canyon

DIFFICULTY: strenuous
DISTANCE: 6.5 miles one way from the East Shore Boat Dock (subtract 2 miles if boat shuttle is used), 5.4 miles one way from the String Lake Trailhead
USAGE: high
STARTING ELEVATION: 6,794 feet; elevation gain, 1,057 feet
SEASON: June through September
MAPS: USGS 7.5-minute Jenny Lake and Mount Moran, WY

This classic Teton hike offers the works: breathtaking scenery, abundant wildflowers, clear mountain streams, wildlife, and dramatic waterfalls. From Jenny Lake's West Shore Boat Dock, a hike of only 1.6 miles takes you through the portals of the canyon to vistas of awesome beauty. The rest of the hike is easy; the trail rises only 600 feet on its 2.9-mile journey through the magnificent canyon. Cascade Canyon's only drawback is its popularity; it is essential to hike early to avoid crowds.

From Jenny Lake, hike to Hidden Falls and Inspiration Point as described in Trips 41 and 42. From Inspiration Point, the trail heads due west through dense forest. In 0.3 mile, the main trail intersects with a horse trail leading to the west shore of Jenny Lake in 0.4 mile. For variety, use this forested, pretty trail on your return to the boat dock. Those who start at the String Lake Trailhead can join the Cascade Canyon Trail via this horse trail (Trip 39).

Shortly after the horse trail junction, pass a rocky, or talus, slope on your right, one of many along the north side of the trail. Furry inhabitants include the indolent yellow-bellied marmot and the tiny, industrious pika. A marmot has yellowish fur on its belly and neck. Listen for their whistles, warning other marmots of your presence. This call earned them the nickname "whistle pig."

Unlike marmots, pikas do not hibernate. They spend the summer diligently gathering plants, scampering to and fro with mouths full of grass. Pikas spread the plants in the sun to dry and later build "haystacks" in dens beneath the rocks. In the dead of winter, pikas remain in their dens, subsisting on their dried bounty.

The talus slopes bear fruit for hungry hikers also. Wild red raspberry can be found among the rocks. Look for berries from late July to September on prickly stems with compound leaves of three to five ragged-edged leaflets. In moister areas of the canyon, find wild huckleberry (a bushy shrub 2 to 3 feet high) and grouse whortleberry (a delicate shrub 6 to 8 inches tall). Both yield delicious reddish purple berries.

Continue west along Cascade Creek. Where the banks are thick with willow, look for moose. Moose relish willow twigs, and many retreat from the warm Snake River bottomland to browse in the cool reaches of the canyon. Often during the summer, moose sit in the shade of the willows. Spot them by looking for the dark horizontal line of their broad antlers among the vertical branches. Watch for moose also on the steep canyon slopes. Despite their awkward physique, moose are skilled climbers.

At about 0.6 mile from Inspiration Point, the canyon opens up in full grandeur. A glacier, moving down the mountain, scooped out this valley to create a flat-bottomed, steep-walled canyon. Its rocks glisten in the sun, "polished" by the tremendous weight and burnishing action of the sliding ice. Above the trail, the peaks rise nearly a mile. The south wall offers Teewinot Mountain (12,325 feet), Mount Owen (12,928 feet), and finally Grand Teton (13,770 feet). To the north stand Storm Point (10,054 feet) and Rock of Ages (10,895 feet).

Arrowleaf balsamroot

About 0.7 mile from Inspiration Point, rockfall from Storm Point dammed Cascade Creek, creating lovely Perch's Pond. This is a wonderful place to rest or wade. Look for rare but beautiful harlequin ducks and common mergansers. Female mergansers are large and handsome, with distinctively crested, bright reddish heads. Harlequin ducks are small, but wonderfully marked. The white, slate blue, and reddish brown male wears his bright colors like a duck who has joined the circus.

The trail continues due west, alternately passing through trees, rock fields, and gorgeous flowered meadows. In July and August, the canyon explodes with color. Delight in red-orange Indian paintbrush, cream-colored columbine, delicate bluebells, purple fringed gentians, yellow goldenrod, and many more. The variety of color and texture is dazzling. Orange, green, and black lichen top trailside boulders. Dark green pines spiral up silvery ledges. Sparkling waterfalls fly down the canyon's south face.

About 3.5 miles past Inspiration Point, look to the south wall (left) for a ribbon of waterfall marking the location of beautiful Valhalla Canyon. Located 2,000 feet above the floor, the canyon is reached only by climbing the steep rock wall beside the water-fall. Once a place of mystical retreat for Native Americans, this canyon is now negotiated primarily by climbers assaulting the Grand Teton. Those bent on exploring this challenging and untrailed canyon must obtain a permit at the Jenny Lake Ranger Station and possess excellent cross-country climbing skills.

About 0.7 mile farther west, Cascade Creek forks. Cross its North Fork on a bridge and arrive in 0.3 mile at the Canyon Fork, a good turnaround point. To the left, the South Fork Trail rises steeply 2,500 feet in 5 miles to reach Hurricane Pass. The North Fork Trail is more popular, rising 1,200 feet in almost 3 miles through meadows and subalpine forest to lovely Lake Solitude (9,035 feet). Lake Solitude is a spectacular destination for hardy dayhikers. In July, glacial lilies rim the lake and the view of the Grand from its north side is unparalleled. The hike is arduous, however, so be prepared. Because of years of overuse, camping is not allowed at the lake, but is permitted about 1 mile below it.

Those returning to the trailhead should retrace their steps.

44

Taggart and Bradley Lakes Loop

DIFFICULTY: moderate
DISTANCE: 4.7 miles round trip
USAGE: moderate
STARTING ELEVATION: 6,625 feet; elevation gain, 650 feet
SEASON: late-May through early October
MAP: USGS 7.5-minute Moose and Grand Teton, WY

Stark, beautiful, desolate, and teeming with life—the loop trail to Taggart and Bradley lakes is all of the above! In 1985 a raging fire denuded the hillsides, revealing the awesome work of glaciers like nowhere else in the park. Don't miss this hike if your family is interested in fire ecology, geology, bird watching, or fishing. For more information, pick up the Grand Teton Natural History Association's informative trail guide, available at the visitor center and from a dispenser near the trailhead. For colorful foliage, try this trail in autumn.

Enter Grand Teton National Park via the Moose Entrance Station and drive 2.7 miles north on Teton Park Road to the Taggart Lake Trailhead and parking lot on the left. Find the trailhead on the lot's west side.

Hike west across dry sage flats 0.3 mile to a fork in the trail. Take the right fork, the shortest route to Taggart Lake. This is prime habitat for playful Unita ground squirrels who pop in and out of holes like furry jack-in-the-boxes. Larger holes (roughly football size) mark the excavations of badgers. Badgers dig elliptical holes resembling the sites of small explosions, with soil and debris spewed in all directions. A badger often appropriates a squirrel's tidy burrow, enlarging it for his wider dimensions after dining on its unlucky inhabitant. Unlike squirrels, badgers are primarily nocturnal and therefore seldom seen.

Sun-tolerant flowers brighten the trail. Prominent are "butter and eggs," with yellow and yolk-colored blossoms arranged on stalks 1 to 2 feet tall (an easy flower for children to recognize); purple rockcrest, a mustard sporting four small purple petals; blue harebell; and creamy buckwheat. The trail soon crosses rushing Taggart Creek and its tributaries. Look west for great views of the Grand Teton. The creek's moister environment supports thimbleberry, wild raspberry, mountain ash, and the following black bear favorites: snowberry, chokecherry, and, of course, bearberry.

The trail rises gently. Pass above a NPS corral, and then head west and follow Taggart Creek. Boulders and shade along the creek provide pleasant resting places. Where there are rocks, look for yellow-bellied marmots. Marmots act like wealthy old tourists, spending the summer eating, sun-bathing, and sleeping. Find them foraging in the early morning, sun-bathing at mid-morning, napping at noontime, sun-bathing again at mid-afternoon, and finally foraging again in late afternoon. By sunset, they are snug in their rocky burrows, asleep.

Throughout this area, the lightning-caused Beaver Creek Fire severely burned over 1,000 acres of 100-year-old forest. Its burning released valuable minerals to the soil, generating a rush of new growth. Snowbrush ceanothus is one pioneer plant growing prodigiously beside the trail. Also known as "varnish bush," it was named for the shiny and sticky coating on its leathery leaves. In early summer, snowbrush bears showy clusters of small white flowers. Native Americans made a soap by rubbing the flowers in their hands with a small amount of water. Today, elk, deer, and moose browse its leaves. Quaking aspen also thrives in the fire-ravaged landscape. Easily identified by its small fluttering leaves and whitish bark, aspen is often the first tree to come back after a fire, for its roots remain alive below the ground. The roots send forth replacement suckers that are nourished by the established root system. Because of the aspen's ability to "rise up from the ashes of destruction," it has been called the "phoenix tree."

Without the usual dense forest cover, hikers can fully appreciate the shape of the moraine they are climbing. About 15,000 years ago, a mammoth glacier rode down Avalanche Canyon (dramatically visible from the shore of Taggart Lake). After thousands of years, it finished its journey and fanned out at the mouth of the canyon, leaving a pile of unsorted rock and soil in front of its eastern edge (a moraine). As temperatures warmed and the glacier melted, the moraine held in the water. In this way, Taggart Lake was created, and in the same way glaciers created Bradley Lake and the other lakes along the base of the Tetons.

At a junction 1.1 miles from the trailhead, the trail levels. Take the left fork that meets Taggart Lake in 0.5 mile. Enter an area where young lodgepole thrive in the full sun. Lodgepole are specially adapted to fire; they produce two types of cones. Their serotinous cones (with a waxlike coating) open only at temperatures above 113 degrees F. The bursting of these cones in a fire produces up to one million seeds per acre!

Life thus returns almost instantaneously after a fire. As timbers cool, birds and small mammals flock to eat the newly released seeds. Many take up residence in standing snags. Look for mountain bluebirds, northern flickers, a multitude of woodpeckers, gorgeous red-headed, yellow-breasted western tanagers, and, atop snags overlooking open areas, red-tailed hawks. Fire-generated openings provide fertile hunting grounds, and tall snags are ideal lookout-posts for the sharp-eyed hawks.

Arrive at beautiful, tree-rimmed Taggart Lake. Dazzling reflections of snow-capped peaks grace its waters. Boulders at water's edge make perfect picnic spots. Gaze up glacier-carved Avalanche Canyon and imagine the path of the ancient glacier. Don't miss Shoshoko Falls visible near the top of the canyon, 2,000

Climbing a glacial erratic

feet above the lake. Try angling for cutthroat and brook trout in the shallow waters. Then follow the trail north along the lake's eastern shore for about 0.5 mile.

To reach Bradley Lake, climb over another moraine at Taggart Lake's north end. On the way, notice aspen with raised black scars. In winter when food is scarce, elk eat aspen bark, occasionally killing trees if they girdle them. The trail rises up and over the moraine, and then switchbacks down to lovely Bradley Lake. Across the lake, U-shaped Garnet Canyon reveals the route of the glacier that created Bradley Lake.

Explore the east shore of Bradley Lake by continuing north on the trail, or start the journey back to the trailhead by bearing right (south) at the next trail junction. Backpackers can find a good campsite on Bradley Lake's north shore. To return home, climb over the moraine, and then hike southeast along its exposed ridge, gaining excellent views of the lakes. After traveling 0.9 mile from the junction, meet the main trail and bear left. The trail follows Taggart Creek back to the parking area.

45

Mormon Row/Kelly Loop

DIFFICULTY: moderate
DISTANCE: 14.75 miles round trip from Moose (12.25 miles from Antelope Flats Road)
USAGE: moderate
STARTING ELEVATION: 6,490 feet; elevation gain, 300 feet
SEASON: mid-May through mid-October
MAP: USGS 7.5-minute Moose, WY

This 14.75-mile bike loop gently courses through open country affording spectacular Teton views. Interesting stops along the way include the picturesque "Shane" cabins and Kelly Warm Springs (bring a bathing suit). En route, watch for coyote, badger, red-tailed hawk, antelope, and even bison. This is an excellent ride for strong young riders, for the elevation gain is minimal. This is also a fine ride for parents towing young children in bike trailers.

Most visitors start from the bike rental store at Moose Village where children's bikes and trailers can be rented. For those who have their own equipment, the preferable starting point is the beginning of Antelope Flats Road, 1.2 miles north of Moose Junction on U.S. 191–89–26. Find Moose 12 miles north of Jackson, off U.S. 191–89–26. To find the bike rental store, take the first right after you leave U.S. 191–89–26 at Moose Junction. To reserve rental bikes (highly advisable), call Dornan's Bike Rentals at (307) 733-2522.

If you're beginning in Moose, ride out to U.S. 191–89–26, and then ride north (left) 1.2 miles to Antelope Flats Road. The highway is very busy, so use extreme caution. (Fortunately, this is the only section requiring highway riding.) To the east is Blacktail Butte (7,688 feet), a prime rock-climbing area. Several local climbing schools offer instruction there for all ages. Some of the trainees hanging 1,000 feet above the highway are preparing for the Grand Teton, where they'll be suspended 5,000 feet above the valley floor!

Turn east (right) on Antelope Flats Road. Stretching out in all directions are miles of dry sagebrush flats. Although the dusty gray-green landscape may first appear uninteresting, sage flats are teeming with life. Its inhabitants include badger, coyote, sage grouse, rabbit, pronghorn antelope, and bison. If you're not familiar with sagebrush, dismount and crush one of its leaves in your hand. It was named for its pungent scent, although it is not related to the herb. Its odorous leaves are a favorite winter food for sage grouse, mule deer, and pronghorn.

This is prime antelope habitat, so keep a sharp watch. Pronghorn are difficult to spot, for their tawny coat and white markings provide perfect camouflage. The pronghorn was named for its branching horns, common to both sexes, although larger on the male. In summer, hidden in the sagebrush are pronghorn fawns (often twins and occasionally triplets), born each spring in late May and early June. On hot days, groups of pronghorns rest in the shade of the sagebrush to avoid overheating. The best time to see antelope in the open is in the early morning and at dusk when they are foraging.

Nevertheless, pronghorn are likely to spot you long before you see them. Their exceptionally large eyes are especially keen; they can detect movement at a distance of 4 miles! When they detect danger, one pronghorn signals to another by raising its white rump hair. Others flare their hairs to spread the signal, and the entire herd disappears in the blink of an eye. A pronghorn can reach speeds of 60 miles per hour and leap 20 feet in one bound! Despite its speed and natural camouflage, the pronghorn's niche in the Greater Yellowstone Ecosystem is far from secure. Its handsome head is a popular hunting trophy, and its favored habitat is endangered by burgeoning residential subdivisions.

Continue east on Antelope Flats Road for 2.5 miles to crumbling cabins on the left side of the road. This is Joe Pfeifer's abandoned homestead, now part of Grand Teton National Park. Joe Pfeifer came to Jackson Hole in 1910 and built these cabins as a summer residence. His intent was to farm, but the quality of his views far exceeded the quality of his soil. Nevertheless, Joe hung on and eked out a subsistence each summer until 1948. The site is locally known as the "Shane" cabins, for the beautifully weathered buildings were used in the classic western film.

Watch the adjacent fields for coyote, who hunt the numerous rodents of the sageflats. Close examination of the ground reveals countless burrows of ground squirrels and badgers. Coyote eat a wide variety of burrowers from shrews to rabbits as well as reptiles, frogs, and grasshoppers.

Continue 0.5 mile east of the cabins on Antelope Flats Road to "Four Corners." To the left (north) the road leads to Teton National Forest. Straight ahead are private ranches. Take a right (south). This pretty stretch of road is easy riding. Relax and enjoy the Gros Ventre Range that lies to the south and east. To the east (left), notice a sign for the Teton Science School. The school is known for its excellent summer naturalist camps for children. Ride for 2.5 miles to another junction signed "Bridger–Teton National Forest Access." This is Gros Ventre Road; turn east (left) to visit Kelly Warm Springs.

Almost immediately look for a patch of green grass and find the pond on the south (right) side of the road. This is a wonderful place for a rest stop. Fed by hot springs originating in the Gros Ventre Range, the water temperature is 75 to 85 degrees F year round. Kelly Warm Springs is a popular local swimming hole and a favorite place for "frogging" (catch and release with nets, of course). The plentiful bullfrog tadpoles reach enormous proportions.

After a swim, ride west back to the main road. Then turn south (left) to continue the loop. Cycle a little over a mile to the small town of Kelly, hosting a small general store with great character. This is a good place to get a cold drink and a candy bar.

From Kelly, ride west. The line of cottonwoods to the left (south) indicates the path of the Gros Ventre River. After 2 miles, arrive at a junction with a gravel road heading north, called Mormon Row.

Turn north (right) on Mormon Row and ride 2.75 miles to its intersection with Antelope Flats Road. Along the way, look for red-tailed hawks perching regally atop tall snags and fence posts. Watch the sky also for their graceful, soaring circles. Mormon Row was named for the settlers who homesteaded this land in the early 1900s.

At the junction with Antelope Flats Road, turn west (left) to return via U.S. 191–89–26 to Moose.

46

Phelps Lake Overlook and Death Canyon

DIFFICULTY: moderate to Phelps Lake Overlook,
   strenuous to Death Canyon

 DISTANCE: 0.9 mile one way to Phelps Lake Overlook,
   3.7 miles one way to Death Canyon

USAGE: moderate

STARTING ELEVATION: 6,770 feet; elevation gain,
   400 feet to Phelps Lake Overlook, 1,461 feet to
   Death Canyon

SEASON: late May through early October

MAP: USGS 7.5-minute Grand Teton, WY

This is a marvelous hike, but it's tough. Even before the 1,000-foot climb to Death Canyon's portals, the trail gains and then loses 400 feet of elevation. Nevertheless, your efforts are handsomely rewarded, for Death Canyon is truly beautiful. Head there to picnic, camp, explore, or look for the plentiful moose who browse the canyon's creek. In summer enjoy the trail's profuse flower displays, and in fall admire its brilliant foliage. For an easier, but still scenic hike, turn around at beautiful Phelps Lake Overlook, just 0.9 mile from the trailhead.

From Jackson, drive north 12 miles on U.S. 191–26–89 to Moose Junction. Turn left and drive about 1 mile to Moose–Wilson Road. Turn left onto Moose–Wilson Road and proceed 3 miles (watch for moose on the left) to a turnoff for White Grass Ranch on the right, also signed for "Death Canyon Trailhead." Turn right (west) and drive 1.6 miles to the parking area. (The pavement stops after 0.7 mile. Cars with low clearance may park at pullouts along the road.) The trailhead is at the parking lot's west end.

Follow the trail west through lodgepole, spruce, and fir. Plentiful water creates a lush garden of flowers and shrubs. Why is there so much moisture here? The answer lies in the origin of the Teton Range. The Tetons were created by a cataclysmic up-lift/sinking along the fault line lying at the eastern base of the range. Along that fault, many thousands of years ago, the valley floor swung downward (as if there was a hinge on the valley's eastern edge) while the mountains swung up. Along the fault there are fissures and, just uphill from the trail, numerous underground springs. The springs bubble up through the fissures and run downhill to water this area.

Is this still an active earthquake zone? One Teton ranger suggested that this park be renamed "Grand Teton National Fault Park!" Experts believe that a significant earthquake along the fault could happen at any time. Historically, major ruptures have occurred every 2,000 to 4,000 years, and the last quake shook about 4,000 years ago. Thus, the question is not *if,* but *when,* another major quake will rock this area.

Along the trail, note the numerous coneflowers, 5 feet tall in midsummer, each with a large brown cone atop a stout green stem. Native Americans used them to treat rheumatism by placing a large quantity in a hot bath. Other tribes boiled their stems to produce a yellow liquid for treating poison ivy. Coneflower was also widely used as an antidote for snakebite.

The trail continues west, climbing gently. Look for purple monkshood on tall stalks. Although it is quite poisonous, Native Americans successfully used monkshood to reduce fever. Today the same chemical is produced synthetically and employed as a heart sedative. In medieval Europe, a closely related flower, wolfbane, was worn on necklaces to ward away werewolves.

Pass huge aspens whose bark has been sampled by elk. Climb moderately to several ancient Douglas fir trees by the trail (300 to 400 years old). Identify Douglas fir by its pendant cones with their distinctive three-pronged bracts between the scales. Switchback up to reach the Phelps Lake Overlook, 0.9 mile from the trailhead. Enjoy the gorgeous view of the large, beautiful lake from this perch 600 feet above the water. Like other lakes at the base of the Tetons,

To Moose Junction

Moose-Wilson Road

To Teton Village

To Death Canyon Trailhead

Ⓣ Ⓟ

JY Ranch

Phelps Lake

Phelps Lake Overlook

Portals

Patrol cabin

N◀

0   1

MILES

Falls

Canyon

Rimrock Lake

Death

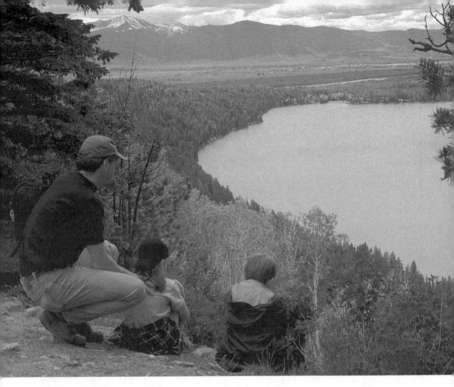

Phelps Lake Overlook

Phelps Lake was created by the movement of a glacier. This viewpoint is located on the edge of its lateral moraine. At the south end of the lake is JY Ranch, owned by the Rockefellers. To the north is the portentous entrance to Death Canyon.

Descend the moraine in switchbacks weaving through aspen and mountain ash. Near the bottom of the moraine, 1.6 miles from the trailhead, arrive at a trail junction. The left fork descends to the lake and to excellent campsites at the lake's north end. Campsites are reached by continuing south 0.2 mile toward the lake. Turn left (east) at the next trail intersection and hike another 0.2 mile. Noncampers stay right for Death Canyon.

Enter pleasingly shady old growth. Pass beneath magnificent Englemann spruce and towering cottonwoods. As you travel northwest toward Death Valley Creek, the trail is enveloped by berry bushes. When the shrubs are full of fruit in late summer, make noise to avoid surprising black bears.

Next ascend steep and narrow switchbacks that climb over 1,000 feet. Strange and alluring rock formations guide your ascent.

Look for the scowling head of a gorilla guarding the canyon entrance. Exposed along the trail are some of the oldest rocks on the surface of the earth. The violent uplifting that occurred eons ago unearthed this ancient stone.

Listen for the "bleat" of pikas on the rocky slope. The tiny "rock rabbits" spend their days gathering grasses and sedges. A 5-ounce pika may gather up to 50 pounds of plants to store for the winter.

Pass a lovely spot by the creek where water cascades over rocks, and wild raspberries and flowers grow profusely. Stupendous views to the east include Phelps Lake and the Gros Ventre Range. Prominent on the eastern horizon is Sheep Mountain (11,200 feet), also called Sleeping Indian for its resemblance to the horizontal profile of an Indian chief with headdress.

At last, follow the creek through an area of large boulders where the trail finally levels. Stroll by clear pools, below sparkling cliffs, along grassy banks and colorful flowers. The effect is paradisiacal.

A little farther down the trail, willows by the creek create superb moose habitat. These immense creatures can eat 50 to 60 pounds of browse per day. Moose eat constantly during the summer for they remain in Grand Teton National Park through the winter when food is scarce. Moose are well-adapted for cold and can easily endure temperatures up to -40 degrees F. Their coat contains a layer of hollow hairs that acts as an effective insulator. Look creekside for moose, but don't neglect the slopes, for moose can climb quite competently. If your binoculars are handy, check the cliffs for human climbers as well.

At approximately 3.5 miles, arrive at a NPS patrol cabin. Just after the cabin, a spur trail to the left leads to a beaver dam. Look for conical tree stumps with teeth marks. At 3.7 miles, pass the junction with the Alaska Basin trail. Stay left to explore Death Canyon.

The level trail travels along the beautiful valley floor. Dense vegetation undoubtedly hides numerous moose. Cross two tributary creeks, and then look for a lovely cascade on your left (south) flowing from Rimrock Lake, over 2,000 feet above the canyon floor. Next arrive at a bridge over the canyon's major creek. For backpackers, the camping zone begins on the opposite bank. This is a good turn-around point for families.

47

Rendezvous Peak/Rock Springs Bowl Loop

DIFFICULTY: strenuous
DISTANCE: 4.2 mile loop
USAGE: moderate
STARTING ELEVATION: 10,450 feet; elevation gain, 1000 feet
SEASON: early July through mid-September (snow may persist into July)
MAP: USGS 7.5-minute Rendezvous Peak and Teton Village

In just 10 minutes, the tram at the Jackson Hole Ski Area rushes hikers over 4,000 feet to the top of Rendezvous Mountain (10,450 feet). It's a painless way (despite a little sting to the wallet) to access a beautiful alpine environment and gain magnificent panoramic views.

Before setting out, heed the following precautions. Hiking at 10,450 feet is very taxing, so take it easy. Since wind and sun can cause rapid dehydration, carry water and extra food for energy. Before hiking, sea-level visitors should first acclimate themselves to valley elevation (6,200 feet). Families with children under 10 may want to limit their hiking to the shorter Cody Bowl trail. Also, bring raingear and warm clothing for the summit temperature is commonly 20 to 30 degrees below that of the valley and afternoon thundershowers are frequent. In addition, sturdy footgear is a necessity, for the slopes are steep and rocky. For information on tram schedules, fares, and trail conditions, call Jackson Hole Ski Resort at (307) 733-2292. Inquire also about the free naturalist hikes in both Rock Springs and Cody Bowl. Rest rooms and a snack shop are located on the summit.

Drive south from Jackson on U.S. 89–191 to the turnoff for Wyoming Highway 22, just south of town. Turn west on Highway 22 and drive about 5 miles; then turn right onto Wyoming Highway 390 (Moose–Wilson Road) and drive 7 miles to the Jackson Hole Ski Area at Teton Village. Turn left into the ski area and drive to a parking lot opposite the clock tower and tram building.

When you buy your tram tickets, ask for the Rock Springs interpretive brochure.

On the tram ride, look for moose on the steep slopes below. Although it may seem unlikely, moose are frequently seen. They climb the mountain to access the willow-choked streams of the canyons and to escape the heat and insects of the valley.

At the summit, exit the tram and head southwest. Pass the Snack Shop and continue southwest along the ridge. Arrive at the junction with the Granite Canyon Trail and descend to the left via the service road where you rapidly lose about 1,000 feet of elevation in switchbacks. Watch for the Rock Springs Bowl trail on the right heading south, at the end of the second switchback. Head right on the nature trail and consult the numbered guide for information on flora, fauna, and geology.

At this elevation, it is critical to avoid stepping on alpine flowers. A trampled alpine garden could take a century to grow back. Growth is slow when the growing season is only a few weeks long each year.

All alpine vegetation struggles to survive by growing close to the ground. Hikers, too, may wish to lay low and huddle together to avoid the wind, even in midsummer. Try a simple experiment with your children. Ask them to crouch down on the trail. They will feel a noticeable difference in the temperature close to the ground, for wind speed increases with its distance above the surface. Increased wind velocity brings greater wind chill and colder temperatures. To survive, alpine flowers must escape the wind because it robs them of heat and precious moisture, and it tears at them with blowing dirt, ice, and snow.

Follow the trail west up Rock Springs Bowl to Cody Bowl. Cody Bowl is the glacial cirque lying just above Rock Springs Bowl. In midsummer, meltwater forms a small lake in the bowl. From Cody Bowl, the trail heads back to the ridge. The ridge gives hikers a chance to experience a stand of *krummholz* (a German word meaning "crooked wood"). *Krummholz* describes trees living at or near timber line whose growth has been stunted by strong winds and severe cold. These trees may be 100 years old, but they stand barely taller than a child. Before leaving the ridge, look east for marvelous views of the rugged Teton Range. To the north is an inspiring view of the Grand Teton. Also visible (from south to north) are Housetop Mountain (10,537 feet), Fossil Mountain

(10,916 feet), Mount Meek (10,681 feet), and Battleship Mountain (10,679 feet). From the ridge, follow the service road back to the tram building for your return trip.

48

National Elk Refuge

> DIFFICULTY: moderate
> ⚙ DISTANCE: 6.8 miles one way
> USAGE: moderate
> STARTING ELEVATION: 6,320 feet; elevation gain, 160 feet
> SEASON: mid-May to mid-October
> Maps: USGS 7.5-minute Cache Creek and Gros Ventre Junction, WY

The National Elk Refuge reveals no elk in summer, but it does provide a nice dirt road with spectacular Teton scenery. Ride in the early morning when car traffic is light and the temperatures cool. At midday, the road can be hot, sunny, and quite dusty. In any season, carry an ample supply of water.

Drive or ride to the National Elk Refuge, located at the east end of Broadway Street, just past St. John's Hospital, 1 mile east of the Jackson Town Square. The Refuge Headquarters provides information on the refuge and is open weekdays, 8 A.M. to 4 P.M. The refuge entrance is just east of the headquarters.

The National Elk Refuge was established in 1912 to preserve the last winter range for elk in the Jackson Hole valley. Prior to its settlement in the late 1800s, the valley supported an immense elk herd, perhaps numbering as many as 25,000. But the town of Jackson and its surrounding ranches took over a large portion of the elk's historic winter range. By the early 1900s, thousands of starving elk wandered the streets of Jackson in search of winter forage. Their population plummeted as they competed poorly with local livestock for winter food. The Jackson Hole Museum displays stark photographs of the plight of Jackson's pre-refuge elk. The winter scenes depicted in the photos moved a concerned public to establish the 25,000-acre refuge which protects about one fourth of the elk's original range.

You won't see elk here in the summer, for they move north in April and early May to their high summer range in the Tetons and South Yellowstone. In late October and early November, the elk return to the refuge. All summer the refuge is irrigated to yield rich grasslands for the approximately 7,500 elk who winter there. When snow covers the grass, the refuge provides alfalfa pellets. A winter visit to the refuge includes a horse-drawn sleigh ride among the herds. In the rarified winter air, it is quite an experience to hear the musical rattling of the elk's huge racks as they spar in the silent, snow-covered valley. Access to the refuge for summer visitors is largely limited to the road. Although some of the refuge's creeks are open to fishing in August and September, many restrictions apply (check at Refuge Headquarters). Hiking and camping are *not* permitted within the refuge. Please obey all signs regarding access, and stay on the road.

Begin the ride by turning left (north) on the dirt road at the refuge's entrance. The good surface makes riding a real pleasure on the first 4.2 miles. Pass the Old Miller Place and ride to the east of sage-covered Miller Butte. At 2 miles, pass a "Nature Trail" where hikers are allowed to climb the slope to examine an elk exclosure constructed in 1993. The exclosure was put up to determine the elk's effect on local vegetation, particularly aspen. Inside the exclosure are numerous aspen seedings, whereas few seedlings survive on the unprotected slope, for the elk love to eat the young trees.

Continue to ride northeast, passing over Nowlin Creek. At 3.6 miles the road curves north and passes Twin Creek Ranch and some private residences. At 4.2 miles from the entrance, county maintenance ends and the road surface roughens.

At 4.5 miles, reach a junction with the Curtis Canyon Road to the right. Go straight (north). The road becomes rougher still as it heads north, but views west to the Tetons are spectacular. In summer, a subtle sprinkling of flowers brightens the dry meadow. At 7.8 miles from the entrance, reach McBride Bridge over Flat Creek.

Flat Creek and other refuge waters support a wild population of Snake River cutthroat trout, a unique variety of the cutthroat species and the only trout native to the area. There are also a small number of brook and rainbow trout. Because of road conditions, the bridge is a good turnaround point for young cyclists. Those who want to continue can ride 2.2 miles farther on fairly rough road to the refuge boundary. To return to the trailhead, just ride the road in the opposite direction.

If fisheries management interests you or your youngsters, a nice side trip is the nearby National Fish Hatchery on U.S. 26–191 just north of the refuge. Holding tanks provide viewing of hundreds of young trout, aquarium tanks display additional species, and friendly hatchery personnel are available to answer all your questions. If your youngsters want to try fishing on the refuge, remember that the refuge's North Elk Park Pond is stocked with Snake River cutthroat and open to youths under age 14. The pond is located on the refuge along U.S. 26–191.

Appendix A
TRIP FINDER

Key to symbols
Handicap access with assistance: (H*)
Difficulty: VE = very easy; E = easy; M = moderate; S = strenuous
Mileage: RT = round trip; OW = one way
Usage: L = low; M = moderate; H = high

Wildlife: Sp = spring; F = fall; • = all seasons
Points of interest: G = geothermal features; SG = self-guided nature trail; P = peak; S = swimming; H = historical interest; W = waterfall

North Yellowstone National Park

	Difficulty	Mileage	Biking	Paddling	Usage	Backcountry Campsite	Fishing	Wildlife	Point of Interest
1. Beaver Ponds Loop	M	5.0 RT			M			Sp,F	
2. Boiling River	VE	0.5 OW			H		•	Sp,F	G,S
3. Mammoth Hot Springs Lower Terraces	VE	0.75 OW			H			•	G, SG
4. Bunsen Peak	S	2.2 OW			M		•	Sp,F	P
5. Blacktail Deer Creek Trail	S	3.7 OW			M	•		•	
6. Children's Fire Trail (H*)	VE	0.5 RT			L				SG,H
7. Yellowstone River Overlook Trail	E	2.0 OW			L			•	G,H
8. Petrified Forest	S	1.75 OW			L			•	H
9. Slough Creek Meadows Trail	E	2.0 OW			M		•	•	
10. Trout Lake	E	0.5 OW			H		•	•	
11. Tower Fall Trail	VE	0.5 OW			H		•	•	W,H

Central Yellowstone National Park

Trail								
12. Mount Washburn	S	3.0 OW		H		•		P
13. Mount Washburn	S	3.0 OW	•	H		•		P
14. Seven-Mile Hole	S	5.5 OW		M	•			W,G
15. Lookout Point to Red Rock Point	E	0.75 OW		H				W
16. Brink of Lower Falls Trail	E	0.75 OW		H				W
17. Clear Lake Loop	M	3.75–6.8 RT		M	•	•		W,G
18. Uncle Tom's Trail	M	0.25+ OW		H				W
19. Artist Paint Pots Trail	VE	0.5 OW		H				G
20. Two Ribbon Trail (H*)	VE	0.75 RT		L		•	Sp, F	

South Yellowstone National Park

Trail								
21. Pelican Creek Loop	E	1.0 RT		L	•	•		S
22. Storm Point Nature Trail Loop	M	3–5 RT		M	•	•		
23. Elephant Back Mountain Loop	M	3.5 RT		M		•	Sp, F	P
24. Fountain Flat and Fairy Falls	E	5.0 OW	•	M		•	Sp,F	W, G
25. Mystic Falls Loop	M	3.2 RT		M			Sp,F	W,G
26. Observation Point	E	1.9 OW		H		•	Sp,F	G
27. Upper Geyser Basin	E	1.5–3.4 OW	•	H		•	Sp,F	G
28. Lone Star Geyser	M	2.3 OW	•	M	•	•	Sp,F	G
29. Shoshone Lake	M	3.0 OW		M	•	•	•	
30. Riddle Lake	M	2.5 OW		L		•		

North Grand Teton National Park

Trail								
31. Jade Lakes	E	2.0 OW		L		•	•	
32. Swan Lake & Heron Pond Loop	E	3.0 RT		H	•	•	•	
33. Hermitage Point Loop	S	8.8 RT		L	•	•	•	
34. Colter Bay	M	4.0 RT	•	H		•	Sp, F	
35. Snake River Float	M	5–6 OW	•	M		•	•	

North Grand Teton National Park, cont.

	Difficulty	Mileage	Biking	Paddling	Usage	Backcountry Campsite	Fishing	Wildlife	Point of Interest
36. Willow Flats Overlook Trail	VE	0.5 OW			H			•	H
37. Schwabacher's Landing Trail	VE	0.5 OW		•	M		•	•	

South Grand Teton National Park

	Difficulty	Mileage	Biking	Paddling	Usage	Backcountry Campsite	Fishing	Wildlife	Point of Interest
38. Leigh & Bearpaw Lakes	M	2.3–3.6 OW			H	•	•	•	S
39. String Lake to Jenny Lake's WestShore	E	1.7 OW			M		•	Sp, F	
40. String Lake Loop	E	3.5 RT			M	•		•	S
41. Hidden Falls	E	0.5 OW**			H			•	W
42. Inspiration Point	E	0.9 OW**			H			•	W
43. Forks of Cascade Canyon	S	4.5 OW**			H	•	•	•	W
44. Taggart and Bradley Lakes Loop	M	4.7 RT			M	•	•	•	W
45. Mormon Row/Kelly Loop	M	14.75 RT	•		M		•	•	S, H
46. Phelps Lake Overlook & Death Canyon	M/S	0.9–3.7 OW			M	•	•	•	
47. Rendezvous Peak/Rock Springs Loop	S	4.2 RT			M			•	P
48. National Elk Refuge	M	6.8 OW	•		M		•		W, F

** One way mileage using ferry

Appendix B
WILDLIFE LOCATOR/SELF-GUIDED WILDLIFE "SAFARIS"

1. WILDLIFE LOCATOR

The following chart lists Yellowstone and Grand Teton's most actively sought-after birds and mammals and describes their habitats and likely locations. Bear in mind that for the great majority, dawn and dusk are the most fruitful viewing times. Another tip for wildlife watchers is to be aware of other viewers. Cars in pullouts (with people gesturing wildly) often means a sighting of some significance. If there's room in the designated turnoff, stop and find out. (But never block the flow of traffic; you may cause an accident!) In addition, park rangers are an excellent resource for information on recent sightings. Most of all, remember to watch wildlife ethically and safely.

Animal	Habitat	Likely Locations: Yellowstone	Likely Locations: Grand Teton
BALD EAGLE	Nests near lakes and rivers. Look in tall trees near water.	Yellowstone Lake, Yellowstone River at overlook (9 mi. north of Fishing Bridge); along Lamar River.	Near Snake River and Jackson Lake. Try Trips 34 and 35. Best bet is a scenic float on the Snake River.
BEAR (BLACK)	Mixed forest and adjacent meadows. Prefers more densely forested areas than grizzlies. In late summer, feeds on berries and whitebark pines.	Along Mammoth–Tower Rd. between Undine Falls and Petrified Tree Turnout; between Tower Jct. and Lamar River Bridge; the Lamar Valley; forest and meadows between Old Chittenden Rd. and Tower Fall; Grant Village area in spring. Be especially alert on Trips 8–10.	West shore of Jenny Lake; forested areas near String, Leigh, Phelps, Bradley, and Taggart lakes. Wide-ranging. Be especially alert on Trips 33, 38–44.

Animal	Habitat	Likely Locations: Yellowstone	Likely Locations: Grand Teton
BEAR (GRIZZLY)	Open country, incl. mountain meadows, open forests, and areas near streams.	High meadows of Lamar Valley; Antelope Creek drainage visible from pullouts on the Canyon–Tower Rd. between Old Chittenden Rd. and Tower Fall; Hayden Valley (overlook 9 mi. north of Fishing Bridge). Be especially alert on Trips 17, 21–33.	Not known to inhabit the park, although bears have been sighted near Emma Matilda/Two Ocean Lake near Teton Wilderness.
BIGHORN SHEEP	Remote and rocky cliffs and mountainsides.	Cliffs above Gardner River east of the Mammoth–Gardiner Rd.; cliffs above Yellowstone River across from Calcite Springs Overlook; on Mt. Washburn via Trips 12 and 13. Try also Trips 5 and 7.	None in park.
BISON	Grasslands and meadows near rivers.	Plentiful in Lamar and Hayden valleys; Pelican Valley. In spring and fall at Upper, Midway, and Lower Geyser basins, and meadows of Firehole Canyon Dr. Try Trips 4, 20, 22, 24–27.	Snake River bottomlands; on Antelope Flats; and along U.S. 191–89–26 from Moose to Moran Jct. Try Trips 37–45.
COYOTE	Primarily grasslands and sagebrush meadows.	Common at lower and middle elevations, especially on northern shore of Yellowstone Lake; in the Lamar and Hayden valleys; and in Upper, Midway, and Lower Geyser basins.	Sagebrush meadows flanking park roads and on Antelope Flats. Try Trips 32, 33, 38, 45.
ELK (WAPITI)	Summer, meadows and grasslands, dusk to dawn, forests in daytime. Spring–fall, throughout valleys.	Meadows of Lamar Valley; Antelope Creek drainage; Gibbon Meadow; Elk Park; and in spring and fall along Firehole and Gardner rivers. Year round at Mammoth Hot Springs. Try Trips 1–3, 19.	Meadows flanking Teton Park Rd., especially west of Timbered Island, southeast of Jenny Lake.

Animal	Habitat	Likely Locations: Yellowstone	Likely Locations: Grand Teton
MOOSE	Near creeks, rivers, ponds, and in marshy areas, especially with willow and aspen.	Willow Park (between Norris and Mammoth); along the northern and northwestern shore of Yellowstone Lake. Try Trips 21, 22, 29, 30.	Along Snake River (especially near Moose Visitor Center, Moran Jct., and Oxbow Bend); at ponds along Moose–Wilson Rd.; and at Willow Flats and wetlands along Christian Creek (near Jackson Lake Lodge). Try Trips 32–37, 43, 46, 47.
PRONGHORN (ANTELOPE)	Open grassland and sagebrush communities.	Along Old Gardiner Rd., from Mammoth to Gardiner; near North Entrance; the meadows around Tower Jct.; along Northeast Entrance Rd. to Lamar Valley. Try Trips 1 and 2.	Grasslands flanking Teton Park Rd. (especially near Timbered Island, south of Jenny Lake), Moose–Wilson Rd., and Antelope Flats. Try Trip 40.
TRUMPETER SWAN	Ponds and waterways.	In fall, Madison River near Seven-Mile Bridge; on Swan Lake off Mammoth–Norris Rd.; along Yellowstone River between Fishing Bridge and Hayden Valley.	Swan Lake (Trips 32 and 33); Christian Pond near Jackson Lake Lodge; Oxbow Bend (Trip 35); and Flat Creek in National Elk Refuge (Trip 48).
WOLF (GRAY)	Meadows, open forest.	Lamar Valley (view from pullouts at dawn and dusk) northwest of the Lamar Ranger Station.	Rare.

2. SELF-GUIDED WILDLIFE "SAFARIS"

The following "safaris" describe eight self-guided driving tours to places where particular animals are likely to be seen. For the best results, try these drives at dawn or dusk. Bring binoculars and keep your eyes moving!

Safari #1: PRONGHORN IN YELLOWSTONE'S NORTHWEST CORNER

From Mammoth Hot Springs, take the Old Gardiner Road (6 miles, one way) through the rolling sagebrush to the park's North Entrance. (For directions, see Trip 1.) The pronghorn make their home in these dry hills. Bring binoculars, and drive slowly, for the antelope's distinctive coloring is effective camouflage. At the end of the drive, turn right to circle back to Mammoth Hot Springs on the park's main road. On the return, look for elk, especially in spring, early and late summer, and fall. In spring, elk cows and their young often gather near the Gardner River. Other animals that may be seen are coyote, bighorn sheep (on the cliffs above the river), and birds of prey.

Safari #2: WOLVES, ELK, BISON, AND BEARS IN YELLOWSTONE'S LAMAR VALLEY

The Lamar Valley is one of the most beautiful and fruitful places to "safari." In spring and fall, large predators are often seen. Drive east from Tower Junction on the Tower–Northeast Entrance Road about 6 miles to reach the beginning of the valley. A series of pullouts on the road's south side provide good places to park and set up spotting scopes. Bison graze in the meadows by the river. Elk are often seen in higher meadows. Scan the upper meadows, especially near the trees (the edge environments) for signs of predators. Wolves and grizzlies frequent the area in the spring and early summer to prey on elk calves. Coyote and bald eagles may also be seen near the river.

Safari #3: BEARS AND ELK IN YELLOWSTONE'S ANTELOPE CREEK DRAINAGE

Antelope Creek Drainage is known for its grizzly bears. Spring and fall are the best viewing times. From Tower Junction, drive south about 6.2 miles on the Tower–Canyon Road to the pullouts overlooking the drainage. From Canyon Village, the pullouts begin just north of the Old Chittenden Road, about 11 miles north of Canyon Village. Elk are usually easy to locate in the meadows. Scan the edge environment for grizzlies. An occasional moose may also be seen. The long viewing distances make binoculars or spotting scopes essential.

Safari #4: BISON, ELK, AND BALD EAGLES IN YELLOWSTONE'S HAYDEN VALLEY

Hayden Valley is the stomping ground for large herds of bison. Visit in spring to see the cavorting calves, or in August to watch the rut's feisty bulls. To find Hayden Valley, drive south from Canyon Village on the Canyon–Fishing Bridge Road about 5 miles. There are numerous pullouts for viewing. At 7 miles south of Canyon and 9 miles north of Fishing Bridge, look for a pullout on the east side of the road. In early summer, when the trout are spawning, this is an excellent spot to see bald eagles. Coyote and elk also frequent the meadows on the far side of the river, visible from the overlook.

Safari #5: BISON ALONG YELLOWSTONE'S FIREHOLE RIVER

Take a drive down Firehole Canyon Drive to see the resident bison herd, usually congregated at the drive's northern end in a meadow near the road. Firehole Canyon Drive is located 15.3 miles north of Old Faithful on the Old Faithful–Madison Road and 0.4 mile south of Madison Junction. With or without bison, the one-way road makes an interesting trip. After watching the herd, ride by 800-foot-high lava cliffs and pass the 40-foot-high Firehole Falls. The popular Firehole River swimming hole, near the end of the drive, is a treat for youngsters. Finally, at the end of Firehole Canyon Drive, pass another 40-foot-high falls, Firehole Cascades.

Safari #6: MOOSE IN NORTH GRAND TETON NATIONAL PARK

It's not hard to find moose in Grand Teton National Park. This safari visits several prime moose habitats, fortunately all in gorgeous locations with superb Teton views. First drive to Willow Flats Overlook, just south of Jackson Lake Lodge. Park in the overlook and look west over the willowed wetlands. Moose love willow and many come to feed in this large, soggy area. If no moose can be seen, walk a very short distance north on the road and look down to the left to the meadows surrounding Christian Creek. Next, return to your car and drive south about 0.5 mile to Jackson Lake Junction. Turn east at the Junction and drive 1.2 miles to the Oxbow Bend Turnout. Park in the turnout and resume your search along the riverbank and wetlands. If moose still elude you, enjoy the incredible wealth of bird life found in Oxbow Bend (see Trip 35).

Safari #7: ELK AND PRONGHORN IN SOUTH GRAND TETON NATIONAL PARK

Throughout the summer, elk and pronghorn are plentiful in the meadows west of Timbered Island at dawn and dusk. To find the "island" (actually a forested hill), drive north on the Teton Park Road about 2.7 miles to the Taggart Lake Trailhead. Just to the north and east, the trees of Timbered Island give shelter and shade to elk and pronghorn during the day. At dawn and dusk they leave the forest to graze on the sage-covered meadows. Drive this section slowly, for the animals frequently cross the road. From the north, start your safari just south of the Jenny Lake turnoff.

Safari #8: MOOSE ON THE MOOSE–WILSON ROAD IN GRAND TETON NATIONAL PARK

Find moose in the ponds along the Moose–Wilson Road at dawn and dusk. You may also see mule deer and elk grazing in meadows by the road. From the Park Headquarters at Moose, drive northwest on the Moose–Wilson Road. The road immediately curves southwest and parallels the out-of-sight Snake River. Try for moose first in the Sawmill Ponds Overlook, about 1 mile from the start of the road. From the overlook, there's a view of several spring-fed ponds. Next continue southwest along the road another mile or so. Ponds and marshy areas, thick with aspen and willow provide perfect moose habitat. Look carefully on the east side of the road. Your safari ends at the turnoff for the White Grass Ranch and the Death Canyon Trailhead, about 3 miles from the start of the Moose–Wilson Road.

Appendix C
Recommended Reading

Build upon your family's experiences in Yellowstone and Grand Teton national parks through excellent books on nature and regional history. The following list includes books that promote an awareness, sensitivity, and enjoyment of the environment. Most are available in park visitor centers.

The Yellowstone Association and Grand Teton Natural History Association are excellent resources for top-quality nature books for all ages. These nonprofit associations sell a wide assortment of books at park visitor centers and through their mail-order catalogs. To receive a free catalog, write the Yellowstone Association, P.O. Box 117, Yellowstone National Park, WY 82190 or the Grand Teton Natural History Association, P.O. Box 170, Moose, WY 83012.

The following organizations also offer nature books by mail: The National Wildlife Federation, 1400 16th Street NW, Washington, D.C. 20036, 1-800-432-6564; The National Geographic Society, Educational Services, P.O. Box 2118, Washington, D.C. 20013-2118, 1-800-368-2728; and The Sierra Club, 730 Polk Street, San Francisco, CA, 94109, (415) 923-5500.

Field Guildes for Children

Alden, Peter. *Mammals—A Simplified Field Guide to the Common Mammals of North America*. Boston: Houghton Mifflin Co., 1987.

Arnosky, Jim. *Secrets of a Wildlife Watcher—A Beginner Field Guide*. New York: Beech Tree Books, 1991.

Magley, Beverly. *Montana Wildflowers—A Children's Field Guide*. Helena, MT: Falcon Press, 1992.

Murie, Olaus J. *Animal Tracks*. Peterson Field Guides. Boston: Houghton Mifflin Co., 1974.

Peterson, Roger Tory. *Birds—A Simplified Field Guide*. Boston: Houghton Mifflin, Co., 1986.

_____. *Wildflowers—A Simplified Field Guide to Common Wildflowers*. Boston: Houghton Mifflin, Co., 1986.

General Nonfiction for Children

Arnosky, Jim. *Crinkleroot's Guide to Walking in Wild Places*. New York: Bradbury Press, 1990.

Bryant, Jennifer. *Margaret Murie: A Wilderness Life*. New York: Twenty-first Century Books, 1993.

The Earthworks Group. *50 Simple Things Kids Can Do To Save The Earth*. New York: Universal Press Syndicate, 1990.

Foster, Lynne. *Take a Hike! The Sierra Club's Guide to Hiking and Backpacking*. Boston: Little Brown and Company, 1991.

Jensen, Kate. *Chief Joseph, Leader of Destiny*. New York: Troll Associates, 1979.

Pollack, Jean Snyder and Robert Pollack. *Common Campground Critters of the Mountain West—A Child's Guide*. Boulder, CO: Roberts Rinehart, Inc., 1987.

Robinson, Sandra Chisholm. *The Everything Bear*. Boulder, CO: Roberts Rinehart, Inc., 1992.

Schneider, Bill. *The Flight of the Nez Perce*. Helena, MT: Falcon Press, 1992.

Picture Books

Arnosky, Jim. *Deer at the Brook*. New York: Lothrop, Lee & Shepard Books, 1986.

_____. *Come out, Muskrats*. New York: Lothrop, Lee & Shepard Books, 1989.

dePaola, Tomie. *The Legend of Indian Paintbrush*. New York: G. P. Putnam's Sons, 1988.

Donahue, Mike. *The Grandpa Tree*. Boulder, CO: Roberts Rinehart, Inc., 1988.

Evans, Lisa Gollin. *An Elephant Never Forgets Its Snorkel.* New York: Crown Books, 1992.

George, Jean Craighead. *One Day in the Alpine Tundra.* New York: Thomas Y. Crowell, 1984.

Goble, Paul. *The Girl Who Loved Wild Horses.* New York: Aladdin Books, 1993.

Lopez, Barry. *Crow and Weasel.* New York: Harper Perennial, 1993.

Plumb, Sally. *A Pika's Tail.* Moose, WY: Grand Teton National History Association, 1994.

Robertson, Kayo. *Signs Along the River—Learning to Read the Natural Landscape*, Boulder, CO: Roberts Rinehart, Inc., 1986.

Seuss, Dr. *The Lorax.* New York: Random House, 1971.

Fiction for Young Readers

Caduto, Michael J. and Joseph Bruchac. *Keepers of the Earth: Native American Stories and Environmental Activities for Children.* Golden, CO: Fulcrum, Inc., 1989.

George, Jean Craighead. *Julie of the Wolves.* New York: Harper & Row, 1972.

____ . *My Side of the Mountain.* New York: E. P. Dutton, 1975.

Mowatt, Farley. *Never Cry Wolf.* Boston: Little Brown and Company, 1963.

Paulsen, Gary. *Dogsong*, New York: Bradbury Press, 1985.

Rawlings, Marjorie Kinnan. *The Yearling.* New York: Collier Macmillan Publishers, 1938.

Savage, Deborah. *A Rumour of Otters.* Boston: Houghton Mifflin Company, 1986.

Thomasma, Ken. Any of the following books published by Baker Book House, Co., Grand Rapids, MI: *Naya Nuki, Shoshoni Girl Who Ran; Om-Kas-Toe, Blackfeet Twin Captures an Elkdog; Soun Tetoken, Nez Perce Boy Tames a Stallion; Kunu: Winnebago Boy Escapes; Pathki Nana: Kootenai Girl Solves a Mystery.*

White, E. B. *The Trumpet of the Swan*. New York: Harper & Row, 1970.

Wilder, Laura Ingalls. *The Little House on the Prairie*. New York: Scholastic Book Series, 1963.

Periodicals for Children

National Geographic World. National Geographic Society, P.O. Box 2118, Washington, D.C. 20013-2118. (800) 368-2728. Ages 8-14.

Ranger Rick. National Wildlife Federation, 1400 West 16th Street NW, Washington, D.C. 20036. (800) 432-6564. Ages 6-12.

Your Big Backyard. National Wildlife Federation, 1400 West 16th Street NW, Washington, D.C. 20036. (800) 432-6564. Ages 3-5.

Zoobooks. Wildlife Education Ltd. , P.O. Box 28870, San Diego, CA 92128. Ages 4-12.

Books for Parents

Brown, Tom, Jr. *Tom Brown's Field Guide to Nature and Survival for Children*. New York: Berkley Publishing Group, 1989.

Carson, Rachel. *The Sense of Wonder*. New York: Harper & Row, 1984.

Cornell, Joseph Bharat. *Sharing Nature with Children,* Nevada City, CA: Dawn Publications, 1979.

Lingelbach, Jenepher. *Hands On Nature: Information and Activities for Exploring the Environment with Children*. Woodstock, VT: Vermont Institute of Natural Sciences, 1986.

First-Aid Books

Gill, Paul G., Jr. *Simon & Schuster's Pocket Guide to Wilderness Medicine*. New York: Fireside Books, 1991.

Lentz, Martha J., Steven C. MacDonald, and Jan D. Carline. *Mountaineering First Aid*. Seattle, WA: The Mountaineers, 1985.

Natural History

Bach, Orville, Jr. *Exploring the Yellowstone Backcountry*. San Francisco: Sierra Club Tote Books, 1991.

Carter, Tom. *Day Hiking Grand Teton National Park*. Garland, TX: Dayhiking Press, 1993.

_____ . *Day Hiking Yellowstone National Park*. Garland, TX: Dayhiking Press, 1990.

Craighead, Frank C. *For Everything There is a Season*. Helena, MT: Falcon Press, 1994.

Craighead, Karen. *Large Mammals of Yellowstone and Grand Teton National Parks*. Yellowstone National Park: Yellowstone Association, 1991.

Eversman, Sharon and Mary Carr. *Yellowstone Ecology: A Road Guide*. Missoula, MT: Mountain Press Publishing Co., 1992.

Fritz, William J. *Roadside Geology of the Yellowstone Country*. Missoula, MT: Mountain Press Publishing Co., 1992.

Harry, Bryan. *Teton Trails, A Guide to the Trails of Grand Teton National Park*. Moose, WY: Grand Teton Natural History Association, 1987.

Marschall, Mark C. *Yellowstone Trails: A Hiking Guide*. Yellowstone National Park: Yellowstone Association, 1990.

Olson, Linda L. and Bywater, Tim. *A Guide to Exploring Grand Teton National Park*. Salt Lake City: RNM Press, 1991.

Raynes, Bert. *Birds of Grand Teton National Park and the Surrounding Area*. Moose, WY: Grand Teton Natural History Association, 1984.

Schmidt, Jeremy and Steven Fuller. *Yellowstone / Grand Teton Road Guide*. Jackson Hole, WY: Free Wheeling Travel Guides, 1990.

Shaw, Richard J. *Plants of Yellowstone and Grand Teton National Parks*. Salt Lake City: Wheelwright Press, 1981.

Wilkinson, Todd. *Yellowstone Wildlife*. Minocqua, WI: Northword Press, Inc., 1992.

Wuerthner, George. *Yellowstone: A Visitor's Companion*. Harrisburg, PA: Stackpole Books, 1992.

Books About Bears

Herrero, Stephen. *Bear Attacks, Their Causes and Avoidance*. New York: Nick Lyons Books, 1985.

Schullery, Paul. *The Bears of Yellowstone*. Boulder, CO: Roberts Rinehart, Inc., 1986.

Appendix D
Conservation Organizations

The following organizations share a common goal of working to maintain and preserve the Greater Yellowstone Ecosystem. All welcome your support.

The Yellowstone Association
P.O. Box 117
Yellowstone National Park, WY 82190
(307) 344-2296

The Yellowstone Association is a nonprofit organization serving Yellowstone National Park and its visitors through support of educational, historical, and scientific programs. The goal of the association is "to educate the public to a better understanding and appreciation of the Yellowstone area and what it represents in terms of our historical and natural heritage." The association publishes quarterly newsletters and serves as a clearing house for a vast number of books, maps, videos, and posters concerning Yellowstone. In conjunction with the Yellowstone Institute, the association sponsors an impressive schedule of multi-day courses on Yellowstone's natural history. As well as helping to support the significant contributions of the Yellowstone Association, association members also receive quarterly copies of the NPS newspaper and a 15 percent discount on publications sold in park visitor centers or ordered through the association.

Grand Teton Natural History Association
P.O. Box 170
Moose, WY 83012
(307) 739-3406

The Grand Teton Natural History Association (GTNHA) operates impressively stocked bookstores in visitor centers in Grand Teton National Park, Bridger–Teton and Targhee national forests, and the National Elk Refuge. Bookstore profits support significant educational, interpretive, and research efforts in the national park and forests. The association also publishes free educational and informational leaflets obtainable within the park. A mail-order catalog of books, maps, and pamphlets about Grand Teton may be obtained by writing to the association at the above address. Association members help support the essential services of the GTNHA to Grand Teton National Park and receive a 15 percent discount on all publications and bookstore purchases.

Greater Yellowstone Coalition
13 South Wilson, P.O. Box 1874
Bozeman, MT 59771
(406) 586-1593

Founded in 1983, the Greater Yellowstone Coalition has grown to more than 6,000 individual members and more than 110 member organizations. Its mission is "to preserve and protect the Greater Yellowstone Ecosystem and the unique quality of life it sustains." The coalition publishes a substantial quarterly newsletter that informs members of regional issues including proposed private developments, governmental actions, wildlife news, and habitat issues. Included in the newsletter are "EcoAction Alerts" aimed at involving the membership in the decision-making process. The coalition also holds annual meetings, outings, educational programs, and provides additional publications. Joining the coalition is an excellent way to keep informed of a wide realm of issues affecting the Greater Yellowstone Ecosystem. For membership information, write or call the coalition at the above address or number.

Jackson Hole Alliance for Responsible Planning
P.O. Box 2728
Jackson Hole, WY 83001
(307) 733-9417

Since 1979, the Jackson Hole Alliance for Responsible Planning has been working to protect the environment of Jackson Hole. Among its environmental successes, the alliance reduced the amount of clearcut logging in the Bridger–Teton National Forest, prevailed in two federal courts to prevent oil drilling in the Gros Ventre Wilderness, lobbied for the establishment of three new wilderness areas, supported long-range planning in Teton County, and participated in major planning exercises involving transportation systems, residential subdivisions, and commercial development. Members receive a bimonthly newsletter, alert bulletins, and invitations to public workshops.

Grand Teton National Park Foundation
P.O. Box 249
Moose, WY 83012
(307) 732-0629

The Grand Teton National Park Foundation is the only non-profit organization dedicated exclusively to raising money for projects that protect, preserve, and enhance Grand Teton National Park. Look for their products throughout the park and in the Jackson Hole area. Your membership will help fund park projects.

Yellowstone Park Foundation
222 East Main Street, Suite 301
Bozeman, MT 59715
(406) 586-6303

The Yellowstone Park Foundation is a nonprofit organization created by a group of concerned citizens, working with the National Park Service, to preserve, protect, and enhance Yellowstone National Park. The Foundation funds projects and programs which are beyond the financial capacity of the Park Service. Without the generous support of private citizens, foundations, and corporations, these projects would be unfunded.

Index

About the Author

Lisa Gollin Evans received her B.A. from Cornell University, then obtained a J.D. from Boalt Hall School of Law. Between books Evans works in the field of environmental law, most recently for the Massachusetts Department of Coastal Zone Management.

Evans believes that respect for and stewardship of the environment grows from a child's positive experiences in natural areas. The best way to create tomorrow's environmentalists is to expose children to the wonders, beauty, and excitement of nature. Her series of guides helps families put her ideas into practice and make the most of their wilderness vacations. Her books include *Rocky Mountain National Park: A Family Guide*, *Lake Tahoe: A Family Guide*, *An Outdoor Family Guide to Acadia National Park,* and *An Outdoor Family Guide to Yellowstone and Grand Teton National Parks*. Evans has also written an award-winning nonfiction children's book, *An Elephant Never Forgets Its Snorkel* (Crown) that was named an "Outstanding Science Book for Children" in 1992 by the National Association of Science Teachers and the Children's Book Council. Another nature book for children will be published in 1997 by Little, Brown and Company. She lives with her husband and two daughters in Marblehead, Massachusetts.

Other titles you may enjoy from The Mountaineers:

An Outdoor Family Guide to Lake Tahoe, Lisa Gollin Evans
Fifty-three short hikes and bike rides within driving distance of
Lake Tahoe. Complete trail descriptions, plus flora, fauna,
history, environmental awareness, safety, and more.

***An Outdoor Family Guide to Rocky Mountain National
Park,*** Lisa Gollin Evans
Includes information on nature walks and short hikes, rainy-
day activities, campground and picnic sites, and best places.

Kids in the Wild: A Family Guide to Outdoor Recreation,
Cindy Ross & Todd Gladfelter
A family-tested handbook of advice on sharing outdoor
adventures with children of all ages and skill levels.

***Glacier National Park and Waterton Lakes National
Park: A Complete Recreation Guide,*** Vicky Spring
The best areas for hikers, bicyclists, boaters, horseback riders,
and skiers. Covers human and natural history, facilities, special
programs, and safety.

Founded in 1906, The Mountaineers is a Seattle-based nonprofit outdoor activity
and conservation club with 15,000 members, whose mission is "to explore, study,
preserve, and enjoy the natural beauty of the outdoors. . . ." The club sponsors
many classes and year-round outdoor activities in the Pacific Northwest, and
supports environmental causes by sponsoring legislation and presenting
educational programs. The Mountaineers Books supports the club's mission by
publishing travel and natural history guides, instructional texts, and works on
conservation and history. For information, call or write The Mountaineers,
Club Headquarters, 300 Third Avenue West, Seattle, Washington, 98119; (206)
284-6310.